In Celebration
of
Simplicity

The Joy of Living Lightly

Penelope Wilcock

MONARCH
BOOKS

Oxford, UK & Grand Rapids, Michigan, USA

First published in the UK in 2009 by Monarch Books
(a publishing imprint of Lion Hudson plc),
Wilkinson House, Jordan Hill Road, Oxford OX2 8DR.
Tel: +44 (0)1865 302750 Fax: +44 (0)1865 302757
Email: monarch@lionhudson.com
www.lionhudson.com

ISBN: 978-1-85424-912-8 (UK)
ISBN: 978-0-8254-6314-3 (USA)

Distributed by:
UK: Marston Book Services Ltd, PO Box 269, Abingdon, Oxon OX14 4YN;
USA: Kregel Publications, PO Box 2607, Grand Rapids, Michigan 49501

British Library Cataloguing Data
A catalogue record for this book is available from the British Library.
Printed and bound in Malta by Gutenberg Press.

Contents

By the same author:

Novels
The Hawk and the Dove (trilogy)
The Clear Light of Day

Short stories
Thereby Hangs a Tale

Poetry
Urban Angel (with Stewart Henderson and Ben Ecclestone)

Spirituality
Learning to Let Go (Lion, publishing 2010)
Spiritual Care of Dying and Bereaved People (Lion, publishing 2010)

Foreword

This is not a 'how-to' book. I don't know how to, or I'd have written it before. It is written with hesitation because I am so often wrong, and because I haven't got it all taped. A hundred times it was started and abandoned, started again, and I was never satisfied. Time and again I told myself this was something to be lived, not written; daily bread to be chewed and tasted, shared and enjoyed, smelt and handled – not a thing to be reduced to words. Besides I find sermons unbearable. Smug saints and gurus, who know the journey like the back of their hands and have nothing left to do but lecture the rest of us, make me stop trying, make me want to get out of the building – die if necessary, if that's what it takes to stop listening to their coy scolding and dreary recommendations.

But I kept coming back to it. Not 'over the last six months', I mean. Over the last thirty-five years. In the course of that time my passion about this has grown until it has become the pattern I am weaving – not perfect, not finished; knotted and muddled in some places, childishly inept in others – my making, that in the end I will offer to the Lord: 'This is what I did with my life. Do You like it?'

And here is what I want to say to you. In case you are looking

Make it your ambition to lead a quiet life, to mind your own business and to work with your hands, just as we told you, so that your daily life may win the respect of outsiders and so that you will not be dependent on anybody.

1 THESSALONIANS 4:9–12
NIV

From the desert of Kedemoth I sent messengers to Sihon king of Heshbon offering peace and saying, 'Let us pass through your country. We will stay on the main road; we will not turn aside to the right or to the left. Sell us food to eat and water to drink for their price in silver. Only let us pass through on foot – as the descendants of Esau, who live in Seir, and the Moabites, who live in Ar, did for us –until we cross the Jordan into the land the Lord our God is giving us.'

DEUTERONOMY 2:26-29
NIV

idly at this page, wondering if this is for you; weighing up whether what's in these pages is important or just bread for the birds, please know this: it works, it's the medicine for today, it transforms life. It's the part of the Bible that shouts off every page but is silenced before it ever gets to church. If you want to follow Jesus, you will need to know and do the stuff in this book. If you don't, you will just be going through the motions.

Writing a book is like sending a message in a bottle. You launch it out from where the waves lap the shore and watch it go; and, for the longest time, that's it. And then, just now and again, someone writes back – and that means so much.

I am asking something of you. If you read this book, and you understand what I mean, and the witness in your heart answers the witness in mine, and the whisper in your soul's core that won't let you rest is the same as the whisper in mine – please – *write to me!* (Letters care of my publisher will find me.) I so long for companions on this journey, because in truth it *is* a strait and narrow way; costly, requiring patience and determination. Walking against the flow of the crowd, out of step with the rhythms of the day; it's a long way home and a lonely way, and I am not always brave and often tired. I have enough people to find me charming and intriguing, enough to tell me gently I don't need to live like this. But if you also have heard the call that I can hear, please write to me and let me know. Tell me what you have discovered and learned on the journey; help me find the next step of the way.

Pen Wilcock

The simple life is one in which there is always time to remember the divine purpose behind each of our tasks, time to listen for a possible divine amendment to the day's schedule, and time to be thankful for the divine presence at each moment of the day.

Lloyd Lee Wilson, Essays on the Quaker Vision of Gospel Order

Grain

When Jesus taught His friends how to pray, He gave them a basics prayer. Bare bones and necessities.

First off – 'Our Father in heaven, Thy Name is holy' – is the necessity to contemplate and adore the loving, wise, divine mystery at the heart of things that breathes light into the everyday and makes life worth living. It's not that God craves worship; God is happy and complete. It's that unless our day centres right from the start on that divine core, we live with an off-centre, dislocated soul. Regardless entirely of what achievements, status and success we may demonstrably have, we don't sit right with the universe unless each day fits in a socket of contemplation and adoration of the holy.

Second base – 'Thy kingdom come, Thy will be done on earth as it is in heaven.' There is an important thing to notice about this. If Jesus says to pray this way, the implication must surely be that we expect a positive result. If you have read the Gospels, you will know that Jesus was not in the business of pipe-dreams. The ending of a prayer is 'Amen' – which means not 'I wish' but 'Let it be'. If we do nothing more with this prayer, let's get this much straight at least: it can be done. In fact, it will be done, because Jesus prayed it – the Jesus who said, 'Lazarus

– come out', and Lazarus came out who had been three days in the tomb; the same Jesus who said to the tempest, 'Calm down', and the tempest came to heel. I, who have had the utmost difficulty calming down even a raging two-year-old or a split congregation, have no idea how he did that; but I believe that he did. So I believe that when Jesus tells me to pray, 'Thy kingdom come on earth as it is in heaven', this is not with a sigh and a shake of the head, as if to say, 'Ah, yes – wouldn't it be nice.' No. This is going to take place. And if it takes place in nobody else's version of earth, it's going to take place in mine. As far as my jurisdiction extends (even if that is no further than the limits of my middle-aged body), I am going to see to it that this prayer comes true; not by might, not by power, for I have none – but most certainly by the Spirit of the Lord. Why else would He tell me to pray it?

And then the request that is the germination-point for this book: 'Give us this day our daily bread.'

I trust this prayer – but what am I asking for?

Our daily bread is the stuff we need to nourish us. It's to fill us up and give us health and energy, and strengthen us and make us grow. Our daily bread is to be tasty and delicious; and if we have it in our pilgrim's bag, all we will need is a wayside spring of fresh water, and we shall be all right.

'Not by might nor by power, but by my Spirit,' says the Lord Almighty.

ZECHARIAH 4:6 NIV

Do not worry, saying, 'What shall we eat?' or 'What shall we drink?' or 'What shall we wear?' For the pagans run after all these things, and your heavenly Father knows that you need them. But seek first his kingdom and his righteousness, and all these things will be given to you as well.

MATTHEW 6:31–33 NIV

… if… thine eye be single, thy whole body shall be full of light.

MATTHEW 6:22 KJV

So this is what we have asked for. And the rest of what follows here is looking with a quiet eye into what that means: what is it that nourishes us, that feeds us? What do we need to strengthen and heal us? What is the nature of the provision we have asked for, the daily bread we beg God to place into the hand we hold out for His gift?

Let's start with the grain.

Bread, whether earthly or metaphysical, is made up of all sorts of things. But the basis – the body – of the loaf is grain.

The grain of this loaf we are making, our daily bread, is simplicity. Simplicity is the body of what will nourish and strengthen us, feed and heal us, give us stamina for the journey. Simplicity is what will continue to taste good when we are sick of life's confectionery and soda and giant steaks.

Can you see and hold this loaf of bread in your imagination? Chunky, dense, brown bread with its sweet, nutty flavour; full of goodness. Bread, the simplest food; for every day.

When people discuss what is the kernel of the Gospel, of course they say 'love' – for Jesus identified love as the one hallmark of a disciple. Former British prime minister Margaret Thatcher once surprised a radio interviewer by describing the essence of

After such a day how sharp your appetite, how good the taste of food! Harriet's brown bread (moist, with thick, sweet, dark crusts) was never quite so delicious, and when the meal is finished you push back your chair feeling like a sort of lord.

'That was a good supper, Harriet,' you say expansively.

'Was it?' she asks modestly, but with evident pleasure.

'Cookery,' you remark, 'is the greatest art in the world –'

'Oh, you were hungry!'

David Grayson, Adventures in Contentment

Christianity as 'choice': and it was a shrewd insight, for the love and trust Jesus calls us to, the faith that gets us on our feet to follow Him, don't just happen to us – they are choices, freely made. Perhaps for an atheist looking on, the key factor would be 'faith', the believer's gift. But I have come to believe that the threshold of the Way of Life is simplicity. We make the choice; we receive the faith; we place our trust in God; we accept the disciplines of love. But the starter-motor is simplicity. If that's dead, we aren't going anywhere.

How Jesus put it, calling a small child to stand in the midst of them, was: 'I tell you the truth, unless you change and become like little children, you will never enter the kingdom of heaven' (Matthew 18:3 NIV).

The entry point is simplicity. No person will make any headway with any spiritual path in any religion unless they go through the way of simplicity, because it is the only way. Unless we change and become like little children, it is just not possible to enter the kingdom of heaven.

Many people say that simplicity is a personal choice (it is, but not in the sense that they mean it – optional); some are called to it, others are not. Soothingly, reasonably, as to a wilful child (my bad attitudes drive them to it, but they're still wrong!), they explain to me that as long as a person has simplicity on

The Lord said, Go out and stand on the mountain in the presence of the Lord, for the Lord is about to pass by. Then a great and powerful wind tore the mountains apart and shattered the rocks before the Lord, but the Lord was not in the wind. After the wind there was an earthquake, but the Lord was not in the earthquake. After the earthquake came a fire, but the Lord was not in the fire. And after the fire came a gentle whisper. When Elijah heard it, he pulled his cloak over his face and went out and stood at the mouth of the cave.

1KINGS 19:11-13 NIV

Any of you who does not give up everything he has cannot be my disciple.

LUKE 14:33 NIV

As servants of God we commend ourselves in every way... poor, yet making many rich; having nothing, and yet possessing everything.

2 CORINTHIANS 6:10 NIV

the morning stars sang together and all the angels shouted for joy

JOB 38:7 NIV

the inside, in the heart, that's what matters – then it's okay to embrace all the trappings of worldliness, because what God looks on is the heart. Unequivocally I refute this. They mean well, but their advice is a signpost that points in the wrong direction. We will make no headway unless we make simplicity *our daily bread* – the physical substance from which we feed in our everyday life.

The grain, the body, the basic material of our daily bread is simplicity. Different people attach different meanings to 'simplicity', though, so I must define my terms or we shall be at cross-purposes all the way through.

The basis for my understanding of Christian simplicity arrived in my life when I came across the stories of St Francis of Assisi when I was fifteen years old. Francis said he had fallen in love with Lady Poverty. He embraced a path of humility and littleness, always willing to choose the smallest and the least, walking barefoot through the world, working with his hands, begging for his bread, seeking the poor as his companions, serving the sick and suffering, and preaching the Gospel by all means – both in word and life. Set free from the insulating layer of possessions that so deadens the spirit, Francis lived very immediately in the natural environment of the living earth. A typical dwelling for him was an abandoned donkey-shed in the forest, or the ruins of a tumbledown church. So he spent a lot of time outside, and became increasingly sensitive to the song of praise the earth is always singing. Every living thing is turned to God in an attitude of adoration. Over the centuries, Christianity has developed a disturbingly materialistic view of creation. Claiming the scripture that humanity is made in the image of God, our theologians have left the text to add a presumptuous article of faith that has no ground at all in the Bible – that human beings alone have souls. On this understanding, believers have felt it acceptable to treat the earth as a combined playground/store-cupboard, there to be plundered and enjoyed with no thought for the consequences. As disquieting rumours of climate change began to be heard, believers thought they were standing firm on the scriptures when they claimed the text in the book of Revelation promising a new heaven and a new earth (so it didn't matter if we ruined the one we already had, completely).

But such is not a biblical faith. The Bible speaks of the (physical, starry) heavens that tell the glory of God and proclaim His handiwork, in Psalm 19. The story of the great flood concludes with God showing Noah the rainbow, and describing it as: 'the sign of the covenant I have established between me and all life on the earth'. So God has a relationship with every living thing; all are known to Him and important to him. The book of Job speaks of the intimate relationship of servanthood and dependency that joins all living things to God. 'Do you send

Praise him, sun and moon, praise him, all you shining stars.

Praise him, you highest heavens and you waters above the skies. Let them praise the name of the Lord, for he commanded and they were created. He set them in place for ever and ever; he gave a decree that will never pass away.

Praise the Lord from the earth, you great sea creatures and all ocean depths, lightning and hail, snow and clouds, stormy winds that do his bidding, you mountains and all hills, fruit trees and all cedars, wild animals and all cattle, small creatures and flying birds, kings of the earth and all nations, you princes and all rulers on earth, young men and maidens, old men and children.

Let them praise the name of the Lord!

PSALM 148:3-13 NIV

the lightning bolts on their way? Do they report to you, 'Here we are'?' asks God of Job (38:35), and: 'Who provides food for the raven when its young cry out to God and wander about for lack of food?' Are we saying that the Bible is mistaken, or speaking metaphorically only, in reporting God describing the raven crying out to Him?

An authentically biblical faith acknowledges that everything that lives has a relationship with God, sings His praises, proclaims His power, and is entitled to a point of view. Therefore an authentically biblical faith approaches the earth and all earth's creatures with profound respect; not as deities, tree-gods to be worshipped or nature spirits to guide us, but as fellow-servants of the living God, made and known and loved by Him, and living to praise and adore Him; as we ourselves are too.

The life of simplicity Francis espoused woke him up to the paean of praise earth is always singing, inspiring him to write the famous *Laudes Creaturarum*, or *Canticle of the Sun*, in which he takes his place in the great chorus of adoration that continually rises from the creation to its Creator.

So it was first Francis, the 'little poor man of Assisi', whose life whispered to me down the centuries, and called me into the way of Christian simplicity and reverence for God's holy Creation.

With the passing of the years I continued to learn, sometimes from the Catholic tradition (the example of believers like Mother Theresa and Dorothy Day, and the witness of the monastic tradition over hundreds of years), and sometimes from Anabaptist witness (Amish, Mennonite, Hutterite and Brethren communities), and sometimes from the lives of individuals who had shaken off complacency and chosen a way of greater clarity, living out in beautiful simplicity their call to follow Christ. I read about the Quakers in their early roots, and modern-day conservative Quakers like Scott Savage; the vision of William Penn; and the Shakers with their wonderful aesthetic of domestic simplicity.

All of them helped to shape my life and understanding, until the call of God tugging at my soul emerged eventually into clearer focus.

This was what the grain of my life, the body of the daily bread I had so often prayed for, was to be.

Christian simplicity, the entry point of the kingdom of God and the basic material of our daily bread, affects our management of:

- Time
- Money

With what shall I come before the Lord and bow down before the exalted God? Shall I come before him with burnt offerings, with calves a year old? Will the Lord be pleased with thousands of rams, with ten thousand rivers of oil? Shall I offer my firstborn for my transgression, the fruit of my body for the sin of my soul? He has showed you, O man, what is good. And what does the Lord require of you? To act justly and to love mercy and to walk humbly with your God.

MICAH 6:6-8 NIV

If we don't change direction soon, we'll end up where we're going.

Irwin Corey

Do not love the world or anything in the world. If anyone loves the world, the love of the Father is not in him.

1 JOHN 2:15 NIV

Where there is no vision, the people perish…

PROVERBS 29:18 KJV

- Possessions

- Speech

- Action (output) and information (input)

- Relationships

- Resources

- Our homes

- Our transport

- The way we dress

As we practise simplicity in a daily walk of faith, its peace percolates through each of those areas. This is not just a hobby, a social trend or a feel-good undertaking. It is a response to clear scriptural imperatives running throughout the Bible as a whole, both Old Testament and New Testament. These imperatives are strongly present in the Gospels, in the teachings of Jesus, where they are central. So we are not talking about minor, peripheral, take-it-or-leave-it issues, but something foundational to being a Christian at all.

The grain of our loaf is this vision of biblical simplicity; the sense of call in all aspects of our life. The vision has to be present. Simplicity is not easy; it requires discipline. We have to pay attention to the detail of life, think ahead, consider consequences and be aware of our environmental and political contexts, in making the choice of simplicity. When we begin the journey, what it asks of us can seem overwhelming, but as we persevere, a wonderful joy of freedom permeates our lives – the sense of burdens lifted, of more spaciousness than we had ever imagined, the light heart that is necessary to walk gracefully in Christ's strait and narrow way.

Christian simplicity means living quietly, in humble, ordinary houses, with as few possessions as we can manage – and those that we have being ordinary, simple things, not status symbols or expensive, luxury items. It means making choices that are socially and environmentally sustainable; sharing by choice the possibilities available to the poorer people in our society. It means choosing clothing that is modest and decent, not swanky or sexually provocative; refraining from stridency, coarseness and aggression in our speech. Christian simplicity involves working with our hands; conscious commitment to sharing; exercising frugality, thrift and good stewardship in our financial affairs – and this stewardship includes recollecting that every purchase we make is a political choice, an environmental choice, and a spiritual choice. 'Bless, bless; and do not curse, purse', I wrote on my wallet when my children were little: they still remember that, now they are grown and responsible for their own finances. In management of money, those who follow the way of Christian simplicity hold in mind the biblical prohibition of usury (lending money at interest): they borrow

Come to me, all you who are weary and burdened, and I will give you rest. Take my yoke upon you and learn from me, for I am gentle and humble in heart, and you will find rest for your souls. For my yoke is easy and my burden is light.

MATTHEW 11:28-30 NIV

No man can serve two masters ... Ye cannot serve God and mammon.

MATTHEW 6:24 KJV

It is no use walking anywhere to preach unless our walking is our preaching.

St Francis of Assisi

Buy things for their usefulness rather than for their status. Reject anything that is producing an addiction in you. Develop a habit of giving things away. Learn to enjoy things without owning them. Reject anything that breeds the oppression of others.

Richard Foster,
A Celebration of Discipline

A religion that takes no account of practical affairs and does not help to solve them is no religion.

Mohandas Gandhi

only when needs must (and when it is the thriftiest option), and then the absolute minimum and repay at the earliest opportunity. They are committed to sharing – their money, their homes, their possessions and their daily life – so that none are in want, everything goes further, and they are not burdened with soul-destroying occupations or steeped over-much in the world. Christian simplicity is mindful that our lives are called to be holy unto the Lord, keeping a wise watch on the gateways of our senses, for we are living temples of the Holy Spirit of God, expected by our Master to choose purity and turn away from inviting or contemplating anything that tends to corrupt us and make us cynical, lascivious or decadent.

Simplicity is the basic material of our daily bread; the first choice. It is the deciding factor – are you going to make this loaf or not? The other ingredients are all there to work with this one basic, central, essential ingredient – simplicity – that is to be at the heart of our daily living.

Yeast

Without yeast the loaf is hard and heavy. Without yeast the bread is solid and daunting, and nobody really wants to eat it.

A friend of mine got her dough kneaded, set it to rise, and then noticed the packet of yeast still sitting unopened on the kitchen counter: the end of *that* project, then!

Yeast is a simple, primitive kind of organism, nothing more than single-cell organisms: but it is a living thing, so it brings life to the dough.

You don't need a lot of yeast to make a loaf of bread rise. You add just a little, and you give it time and warmth, and it works through the whole batch, lifting it up out from being a sullen mass to the light, pliable mixture that will make delicious bread.

The way of simplicity can seem very daunting, especially when it is defined in negatives: but there are some ingredients to add that make it light and manageable. Like yeast, these are only humble, simple, basic things – but what a *difference* they make! They bring the way to life; transforming it from heavy going, to a path of light heart.

Angels can fly because they can take themselves lightly.

G. K. Chesterton

We have different gifts, according to the grace given us. If a man's gift is prophesying, let him use it in proportion to his faith. If it is serving, let him serve; if it is teaching, let him teach; if it is encouraging, let him encourage; if it is contributing to the needs of others, let him give generously; if it is leadership, let him govern diligently; if it is showing mercy, let him do it cheerfully.

ROMANS 12:6–8 NIV

A cheerful look brings joy to the heart, and good news gives health to the bones.

PROVERBS 15:30 NIV

Cheerfulness is the atmosphere in which all things thrive.

Jean Paul Richter

Common sense and a sense of humour are the same thing, moving at different speeds. A sense of humour is just common sense, dancing.

William James

Your focus determines your reality.

Qui-Gon Jinn
(Star Wars I)

Here are the ingredients that leaven the lump:

- Cheerfulness

- Humour

- Imagination

You need only a little, but it has to be mixed right through. These ingredients are nightmarish if you add them by the spadeful!

Cheerfulness becomes wearing, grating, when it is relentless. We do need companions who have stillness and seriousness about them, whose kindness is earthed by the gravity of peace; but moodiness, touchiness and resentfulness sour the core of our life together. Time and again, a cheerful attitude restores our perspective, comforting us, lifting the atmosphere, bringing a light touch that makes daily chores into pleasant and purposeful work.

Humour becomes exasperating and isolating when every question or observation is countered with a quip or a clever remark. When it is overdone, humour creates an insulating layer that prevents intimacy and so becomes destructive. To be able to trust someone, you have to be sure they will not make a joke of your vulnerability, the tender and unprotected truths of your soul that you have confided in them. But the way of simplicity is so counter-cultural that they who cannot laugh at themselves will not travel far along it. When times are grim – in poverty or illness or walking in the valley of the shadow of death – sometimes the only thing that will lighten the heaviness and darkness is a sense of humour.

Imagination becomes neurosis when it takes leave of reality. Poor Clare nuns speak about our minds being 'recollected' – having a consciousness that is focused, not scatty. They make a moment by moment practice of mindfulness; the ability to be present to now reality, to bring to this moment a quality of real attention. When I think about it, I can so vividly recall to mind my mother's voice, and the various phrases that guided me as a small child: 'Pay attention!… Look what you're doing!… Look where you're going!… Concentrate!' What a wise lesson to have taught me.

The way of simplicity requires that we cultivate a practical, focused approach, able to bear in mind our choices and intentions, and able to attend to our tasks properly. This is necessary if we are to steward time and money faithfully; we squander both when we lose ourselves in fantasies about the image we are projecting, or permit ourselves to be absent-minded.

But without imagination, the daily reality of Gospel simplicity

We have no money. Now we must think.

George Washington
at Valley Forge

Hard work is the leaven that raises the dough.

Source unknown

Apathy can be overcome by enthusiasm, and enthusiasm can only be aroused by two things: first, an ideal, which takes the imagination by storm, and second, a definite intelligible plan for carrying that ideal into practice.

Arnold Toynbee

would become very dull. Imagination adds the creativity that leavens our experience of simplicity.

Amy Dacyczyn, the creator of the wonderful *Tightwad Gazette* (the journal, now available in book format, that inspired and connected a whole movement of people achieving personal freedom through frugality and thrift), describes delightfully imaginative approaches to thrifty birthday treats. On one occasion the family's barn became the setting for a pirate ship constructed from household items creatively rerouted from their ordinary courses in honour of the special event. Amy's son celebrated his birthday with a gathering of pirates whose evening set sail on that ship. On her daughter's birthday, a room was prepared as an elegant restaurant. The birthday girl and a friend arrived dressed to the nines, to be greeted by the *maître d'hôtel* (Dad) and a waitress (Mum) ready to present the menu (choice pre-arranged!) and wait upon them through the evening.

In my own family, buying gifts for birthdays and Christmas has been supplanted by handmade presents: an anthology of poems and pictures; a crocheted blanket; an appliquéd laundry bag; a piece of calligraphy; a story written, illustrated and bound into an entirely original and individual book.

Just as imagination leavens simplicity, so also simplicity

> It's not funny at all that we do all that advertising for children. Why is advertising for children allowed? What possible reason can there be for having those effing adverts on ITV for all this crap that's made by poor people in poor countries that we sell our children who have too much?
>
> Emma Thompson

> One reason I don't drink is that I want to know when I am having a good time.
>
> Lady Astor

strengthens imagination. At first, we cannot imagine how we might pass the time when we turn off the TV… or abstain from that addictive consumerist leisure activity – shopping… or have no more use for pamper parties or night-clubbing or evenings at the pub. For many of us, the idea of a social gathering without the blur and hype and bonhomie contributed by alcohol is unthinkable: but once we come home to ourselves and, in the spaciousness of simplicity, relax and become comfortable with who we are, tea or juice is fine, and soda is a treat for special occasions, and we learn that to be just ourselves is enough. Simplicity rescues us from loneliness, from the isolation of taking refuge in public image and false persona.

Simplicity is a strait and narrow way, to be sure, but it is also a path of astonishing freedom.

The action of yeast in the dough is to create lightness and volume, incorporating air. Yeast brings spaciousness.

We sometimes make the mistake of perceiving space as nothing. We conceptualize space as a container-in-waiting, as emptiness to be completed by the addition of an item – 'What are you going to put on that shelf? What shall we display on the mantelpiece?' This is the prevailing attitude of our culture, and it is worth saying that the choice to live simply can cause a certain amount of friction as a result.

True individual freedom cannot exist without economic security and independence.

Franklin Delano Roosevelt

Thirty spokes share the wheel's hub. It is the space at the middle that makes it useful.

Lao Tsu

Keep falsehood and lies far from me; give me neither poverty nor riches, but give me only my daily bread. Otherwise, I may have too much and disown you and say, 'Who is the Lord ?' Or I may become poor and steal, and so dishonour the name of my God.

PROVERBS 30:8-9 NIV

The ability to simplify means to eliminate the unnecessary so that the necessary may speak.

Hans Hofmann

Living simply is of itself a work of art: it is beautiful. Life lived with intentional simplicity radiates calm and order, so even if accomplished for no more than its own sake, it would still be a balm, a salve, to our frantic, stressed, over-pressured society. But Gospel simplicity is not for its own sake, but is a way of worship and service. The purpose of Gospel simplicity is to create the space necessary for us to obey the call of Christ: 'follow Me'.

Following Jesus is not just a matter of acquiescence to doctrines, but implies an active transformation of our lives: that is to say, it is not only something we believe (though it starts with that), but also something we do because of what we believe.

Christian faithfulness requires that we:

- Pray and wait quietly upon the mystery of God's presence.

- Make ourselves available for loving service of others, acting as conduits of God's healing and peace where that is needed.

- Become aware of the implications of our engagement in society: what happens to the money we spend in the shops; the ethical journey of the products we have purchased; the environmental, social and political impact of the choices we make as citizens – not just in how we vote, but how we shop and how we source our goods and services.

- Live debt-free lives and live in such a way that we encourage debt-free societies – which sometimes means accepting lower wages or financial returns in our own lives.

- Ensure that our homes and businesses reflect the peace and order of heaven. We should not live in a hurry, all rush and tear; or in a muddle, fragmented and chaotic. The daily work of our minds and hands should hum along quietly, our hymn of praise offered up in gratitude for the grace that includes us and creates the opportunity for our contribution.

It takes very little reflection to see that such practice of our faith cannot be done in a rushed, multi-tasking manner, but requires an emphatic prioritizing of quality over quantity. It means that we learn to envision our every choice and action as an active component of our relationship with God: there is no compartment labelled 'Doesn't Really Matter'. Everything matters: from the tone of voice with which we speak to our partners and children, to the separation of our trash for responsible disposal, to our body language and the expression on our faces and the kind of car we drive – all of it is part of

You can't force simplicity; but you can invite it in by finding as much richness as possible in the few things at hand. Simplicity doesn't mean meagreness but rather a certain kind of richness, the fullness that appears when we stop stuffing the world with things.

Thomas Moore

To live content with small means; to seek elegance rather than luxury, and refinement rather than fashion; to be worthy, not respectable, and wealthy, not, rich; to listen to stars and birds, babes and sages, with open heart; to study hard; to think quietly, act frankly, talk gently, await occasions, hurry never; in a word, to let the spiritual, unbidden and unconscious, grow up through the common – this is my symphony.

William Henry Channing

the dialogue that is always going on between ourselves and our Maker at the intimate core of our being.

> What's the use of a fine house if you haven't got a tolerable planet to put it on?'
>
> Henry David Thoreau

If we buy organically grown food free of excess packaging, our life becomes a psalm of blessing that will bring prosperity to our fields. If we shop at small, local, family businesses, enriching the folk who will in turn spend that money locally, we are living a silent prayer of blessing over our local community. If we drive small, economical vehicles (only one per family), our lives are saying to God that we love this beautiful earth, and don't want to pollute it. If we choose fairly traded goods, we are showing God that we have heard His call to love our neighbour and mean to take it seriously. If we live in an orderly manner, building in availability and thinking/listening time, we are choosing the prophet's way – a life that looks up to God in obedience, saying, 'Here am I, send me'; saying, 'Speak, Lord, your servant is listening', *and meaning it.*

> *'What shall I compare the kingdom of God to? It is like yeast that a woman took and mixed into a large amount of flour until it worked all through the dough.'*
>
> LUKE 13:20-21 NIV

We can achieve all this only if we steward the time we have been given by a daily discipline of simple lifestyle. When we choose simplicity, we are in effect becoming the yeast in the dough that Jesus likened to the kingdom of heaven – we are introducing spaciousness.

As we free ourselves from the entanglements of too many possessions, and from over-committing our time and money, a lightness begins to breathe through our lives, a kind of quietly exuberant joy – it really is like the bread-sponge rising as the yeast works away silently upon the grain.

Yet the discipline of simplicity is a planet with a moon – the discipline of setting and keeping boundaries. In these rushed and pressured days, so many people are almost frantic – trying to achieve too much with too few resources and too little time, trying to cram too much into too little space.

Imagine a house as just a box to keep out the weather (though a home is more than that, to be sure; a home is a sanctuary of love). It would not take a very big box to house a human being. Add a bed with a quilt and pillows, a stove for warmth and cooking, a cupboard for essential pots and pans. Put a row of hooks on the wall for a coat, a wash-bag, a towel. Add a sink, some boots by the door, a clock, a laptop and a mobile phone. Hang a lamp from the ceiling, and add a set of shelves for groceries and favourite books and writing essentials. Add a fridge-freezer, and a bag of tools. That house-box need not be very big. A person with such requirements would have little expenditure and take up little space.

But add a bulky three-piece suite, two or three coffee-tables, a standard lamp and some table-lamps, a dining-table and chairs, 'best' cutlery and crockery for guests, several large clothes

I like to walk about among the beautiful things that adorn the world; but private wealth I should decline, or any sort of personal possessions, because they would take away my liberty.

George Santayana

Too many people spend money they haven't earned, to buy things they don't want, to impress people they don't like.

Will Rogers

closets, a clothes dryer, a television, a cabinet for drinks and glasses, a microwave oven, a bread-maker, an icecream-maker, a second freezer, a toaster, several suitcases, a sound system, a desktop computer and associated furniture, a guest bedroom, several chests of drawers, five more large bookshelves, a closet full of spare bed-linen, an extra bathroom, a rowing machine and an exercise bike, a forest of ornaments and thirty-five years' worth of hoarded memorabilia – and you need a mansion!

It seems inappropriate to me that a person should dedicate years of working life, paying thousands of pounds in interest payments to a mortgage company, in order to secure accommodation *not for themselves but for their furniture*!

Choosing simplicity allows us to scale down or eliminate debt, which in turn gives back to us our choices of how we may use our time, and frees us from the responsibility of endlessly acquiring and maintaining inanimate objects.

As soon as we begin to do this, freeing up space in our lives so that we have more time, more space and more money, we immediately begin to attract the attention of overburdened people who have not so chosen. A light kindles in their eyes as they realize that we can be annexed to their lives as a resource – so that our time, space and money, being now free, can be used to run their errands, accommodate their overflowing hoard and pay their debts.

It would surpass the powers of a well man nowadays to take up his bed and walk, and I should certainly advise a sick one to lay down his bed and run.

Henry Thoreau: *Walden*

Dave Michael Bruno, on his excellent blog, *www.guynameddave.com*, wrote about his 100 Thing Challenge, in which he set himself the challenge of reducing his personal stash of possessions (not counting books, tools or family and household items) to a total of 100 things. The 100 Thing Challenge is now on Facebook, and a book is on the way.

What would be on your list of 100 things?

Very quickly we learn that unless we add, to the discipline of simplicity, the discipline of boundaries, we shall not only be back to square one but held there until the permission of another gives us leave to move on – for it is even harder to get rid of someone else's stuff than your own.

I have more than one friend whose house is used for storing the possessions of several relatives whose own living arrangements offer insufficient accommodation for their accumulated stuff.

We are mistaken when we assume that inanimate objects have no life of their own; on the contrary, we become slaves to our possessions, giving our time and wealth to nurture and house them. We are mistaken when we think that a space is just an emptiness awaiting an object. 'Nothing' is, in fact, something.

As we prune and thin out our possessions, not only does it create lightness of being, but it enables us to see how the daylight and moonlight enter our homes, see the architectural structure of the house itself, watch how the light moves through space during the day. We become more centred and less stressed, our actions becoming movements of peace – so our health improves. It becomes once more possible to dust and sweep without this being an onerous task, now the house is free of clutter; and once the dusts and moulds and parasites are dealt with, our health improves again. With all that stuff gone, our spare

John Maeda, in his brilliant book *The Laws of Simplicity*, writes of a friend who volunteers at a shelter for poor people at the end of their lives. Each one has a single bedside shelf, holding the sum of their worldly belongings – a ring, a photo, a keepsake...

If you were a resident of that shelter, what would you have on your shelf?

Besides the noble art of getting things done, there is the noble art of leaving things undone. The wisdom of life consists in the elimination of non-essentials.

Lin Yutang

K.I.S.S.

(Keep It Simple Sweetheart)

> *Godliness with contentment is great gain.*
> *For we brought nothing into the world, and we can take nothing out of it.*
>
> 1 TIMOTHY 6:6 NIV

room becomes actually spare again – we share our home with a lodger, and the rent allows us to free ourselves of mortgage debt or make ethical choices in our grocery shopping.

Mammon, the god of power, status, acquisition and greed, is a hard taskmaster. It's nice to be free.

Herbs

Not everybody adds herbs to bread, but for me it's not quite complete without them. Thyme is the bread herb, and I like to go outside where the thyme grows fragrant in the border, and cut some fresh to mix in with the dough.

Herbs are medicinal and also delightful. Their aroma is just heavenly, and always lifts my mood: so herbs are therapeutic on two levels.

I have always been an enthusiast for herbs. When I was a girl, helping my mother in the kitchen, she'd exclaim, 'Not too many! You're not making a poultice!'

'Too many' was not a meaningful concept for me where herbs were concerned. How can you have too many herbs? In the house where we live now, when we arrived the garden was grassed over for children to play. Tony, my husband, set about making flower-beds and veggie-beds, putting in a pond and apple trees; and our daughters helped him put up the greenhouse.

'What do you want to plant?' he asked me. 'Rosemary… sage… lavender… thyme… golden oregano…' came my inevitable reply, 'and a tree.'

And God said, 'Let the He bringeth forth grass for the cattle, and green herb for the service of men;

PSALM 104; BCP

And God said, 'Let the earth bring forth grass, the herb yielding seed, and the fruit tree yielding fruit after his kind, whose seed is in itself, upon the earth: and it was so. And the earth brought forth grass, and herb yielding seed after his kind, and the tree yielding fruit, whose seed was in itself, after his kind: and God saw that it was good.

GENESIS 1:11–13 KJV

For there is hope of a tree, if it be cut down, that it will sprout again, and that the tender branch thereof will not cease. Though the root thereof wax old in the earth, and the stock thereof die in the ground; Yet through the scent of water it will bud, and bring forth boughs like a plant.

JOB 14:7–9 KJV

God has cared for these trees, saved them from drought, disease, avalanches, and a thousand tempests and floods.

But he cannot save them from fools.

John Muir

Human ignorance is largely to blame for the floods and droughts of recent years, in particular our ignorance about the way water passes through the landscape. Trees slow down the movement of water, and circulate it in the area where they are planted. Their great root systems stabilize the earth, and trees both attract and absorb the rain. They return moisture to the air, and take up moisture from the earth. Wherever plants are growing, rainfall can soak into the ground, and moisture is captured and released slowly. When we cut down the trees and pave everywhere, building roads and laying down concrete surfaces, we create both droughts and floods. The rain cannot soak into the earth, so flash floods result from rainfall while the buried ground remains dry. Green things are urgently needed to avert human catastrophe.

A politician once told me kindly, 'I think human beings are more important than trees'; and this is the epitome of ignorance. Even if we were motivated by nothing but pure selfishness and interest in our own well-being, even then, the best thing we could do would be to plant trees. The trees are the lungs of the earth. We need them; it's that simple.

Human beings are not somehow separate from the rest of creation, though certainly we have a specific, God-ordained role to play within it. Because we are part of the living earth, it completes us. We should therefore approach the earth with humility; understanding that the trees, the flowers, the green plants are necessary for our healing and well-being. It was not casual or accidental that the ancient Hebrew writers, under inspiration from God, envisaged Adam and Eve in a garden. One of the most positive and prophetic things an ordinary person can do in our day is plant a garden.

So we hadn't lived long in our new home when I asked Tony if he would be happy for me to take up the paved hard standing for car parking at the front of the house, and turn it back into a garden again. As he is our main gardener, I wondered if I might have this patch for a garden of my own. He asked me what I would plant. 'Rosemary… sage… lavender… thyme… golden oregano…' I replied, 'and roses, pinks, geraniums, nasturtiums… and a small tree.' People passing by will feel God touch them in the beauty and the fragrance of our herbs. They will be a place of blessing and healing, where before there were only concrete, dust and discarded food wrappers blown by the wind.

Sometimes among friends on retreat, I may ask the question, 'Where is it that you feel closest to God?' I can guarantee you that wherever that question is asked, there will be few who say 'in church', and many who say 'in the woods… in the fields… in my garden… by the sea…' The beauty of the natural world heals and restores us, and it seems that God still comes looking

God said, Behold, I have given you every herb bearing seed, which is upon the face of all the earth, and every tree, in the which is the fruit of a tree yielding seed; to you it shall be for meat. And to every beast of the earth, and to every fowl of the air, and to every thing that creepeth upon the earth, wherein there is life, I have given every green herb for meat: and it was so.

GENESIS 1:28–31 KJV

for us in the garden, as He came looking for Adam long ago. However lost we have become, however estranged from ourselves, if we take time to sit in the garden as evening falls, God comes walking, and asks us again, 'Earthling, where are you?' And we have the chance to say, 'Lord, here I am.'

As we mix the ingredients for the good bread of our lives, I think it makes sense to remember the herbs.

Herbs add the aesthetic qualities of their fragrance and flavour, and their therapeutic qualities.

When Jesus healed people, He described them not as having been cured, but as having been made whole. He addressed their whole being – body, mind, heart, will, soul and spirit. The words 'holy' and 'healthy' come from the same root (just as 'salve' and 'salvation' do). The Old English greeting from which the modern 'hallo' came, was '*wes hal*' ('be thou whole'). There is a two-way flow to this. On the one hand, holiness is necessary for health and well-being: real peace and joy and contentment are found in walking in the way of holiness. It is said by some that all illness has an emotional root; and since we cannot be divided into compartments, it is bound to be the case that all physical illness has an unseen component (emotional or spiritual). Put simply, being ill and in pain makes us unhappy; and being unhappy also tends to make us ill. As we observe the two-way flow, and hear Christ's words, 'be thou whole', we begin to realize that it follows from this that health is therefore a duty of holiness. It is part of our discipleship to inform ourselves about what promotes health for ourselves, the community and the whole of creation – *and then do it*! It is part of our discipleship to take exercise, to eat wisely, to rest enough, and to work towards ensuring that everyone has clean air and water, and that the earth is cherished and nourished, not polluted and trashed. 'Be thou whole' should breathe from our lives as surely as it did from Christ's.

Living simply is crucial to this aspect of our society. It is very difficult to live healthily without simplicity. I have lived with more than one friend who likes to accumulate possessions, and I have noticed this: such people do not clean. The corners of their home are never washed or swept; under the bed where junk is stuffed, fluff and dust accumulate. Cat sick is left to soak into the carpet. Mildew grows in abandoned coffee cups down on the floor by the sofa. Moulds accumulate on walls against which piles of dirty clothes are stacked. Respiratory disorders, infections, pests and parasites are the result. Such housekeeping does not honour and invite Christ's blessing, 'be thou whole'.

Cluttered timetables and over-eager pursuit of financial gain also prevent Christ's blessing, 'be thou whole', from permeating

The statutes of the Lord are right, rejoicing the heart: the commandment of the Lord is pure, enlightening the eyes. The fear of the Lord is clean, enduring for ever: the judgments of the Lord are true and righteous altogether.

PSALM 19:8–9 NIV

Cleanness of body was ever deemed to proceed from a due reverence to God.

Francis Bacon

Slovenliness is no part of religion. 'Cleanliness is indeed next to Godliness'.

John Wesley

our lives. Stressed, irritable, too tired to cook or to go for a walk, beside themselves with exhaustion and burdened with debt and anxiety, those who have chosen Mammon's way comfort themselves with useless purchases of toys and gadgets, diversions and ornaments, and take refuge in processed food – half of which is thrown away. It is impossible to be happy with too much to think about and too much to do; and no one can be said to be whole, who is not happy.

The way of simplicity is both healing and beautiful. Just as green and growing things slow down the movement of water through the landscape, so simplicity slows us down, allowing us to savour and experience life's challenges, encounters and blessings.

The aroma of herbs is different from the fragrance of flowers. It is clean and sharp, medicinal; and it creates well-being, lifting the spirits and cheering the heart. The varying flavours of different herbs add personality and character to the bread.

Likewise, simplicity is clean and sharp; purposeful and wholesome. It remedies the ailments of decadence. People drowning in consumerism, obsessed with their image, assessing the worth of all things by their price ticket, jaded and anxious and easily bored, are healed by simplicity.

Health is a state of complete physical, mental and social well-being, and not merely the absence of disease or infirmity.

World Health Organization, 1948

If you have health, you probably will be happy, and if you have health and happiness, you have all the wealth you need, even if it is not all you want.

Elbert Hubbard

Working with our hands, we rediscover the flavour of creativity. The high streets and shopping malls of the big cities are almost interchangeable – the same array of chain stores, selling the same identical mass-produced products, face us in every one.

When gifts and clothes and food are handmade with love, individuality and personality are recovered. When one of my daughters gives her sister a story she has written, made into a book she has printed at home and illustrated herself, bound by hand using recycled card and fabric scraps, she has upgraded her giving from pricey to priceless.

Surfeited with affluence, bored and tired and irritable, looking for trouble in their personal relationships, trying one counsellor after another in search of elusive answers, so many people no longer even know what they are looking for.

When the sharp, clean fragrance of simplicity gets to work on their lives, they begin to wake up again. As they make the transition from clutter to space; from chaotic over-commitment to life lived on purpose, one thing at a time; as they emerge from dependence on machinery to working with their hands and travelling on foot – they come alive again.

It is said that whatever you take refuge in also takes refuge in you: whatever you allow to fill your consciousness ultimately

My own prescription for health is less paperwork and more running barefoot through the grass.

Leslie Grimutter

Life is no brief candle to me. It is a sort of splendid torch which I have got a hold of for the moment, and I want to make it burn as brightly as possible before handing it onto future generations.

George Bernard Shaw

Everyone who winds life round a core of machinery – physical machinery or social machinery , lie schools and institutions and global corporations – is affected profoundly , and comes inexorably, I believe, to be a servomechanism of the machinery he or she excessively associates with.

John Taylor Gatto

There is no memorial to the first human worker who was superseded by a machine. The significance of events like these at the time tends to be easily overlooked.

David Whiteland

The machine does not isolate man from the great problems of nature but plunges him more deeply into them.

Antoine
de Saint-Exupery

comes to dominate you. A clear example of this is the spreading epidemic of obesity in our unhappy society starved of meaning and connection: people take refuge in fat, with the result that fat takes refuge in them.

Increasingly human beings are taking refuge in machines: stop for a moment and let your mind run through your home and your day. How much of it depends on machines? How do you communicate with others most often? How do you get your groceries? How do you store your food… clean your home… prepare your food… wash and dry your clothes… keep warm… tend your garden… travel… make music… relax in the evening? Are machines involved in any of these? If you are like most of us, *all* those aspects of your life have been turned over to machines.

Undoubtedly machines are useful; they amplify what we can achieve immensely (though we are sometimes baffled to discover that far from speeding things up, machines leave us with less time than we had without them).

Machines, unlike living beings, are defined in terms of function: they are self-contained in their own isolation, unable to initiate, relate or create. They can only carry out what they have been programmed and instructed to do: and often, once the command has been given, the process cannot be stopped.

What we take refuge in also takes refuge in us. As we rely increasingly on machines in every aspect of our life, including our communication with others, so in time our social structures and interactions take on an uncanny resemblance to machinery.

We begin to develop the isolation of machines, too. We step out of our homes and into the car to go to church or the office or the mall. Living this way, we see only what we have selected; who and what we will meet become predictable. In the church, increasingly, the people have forgotten how to play musical instruments – and are glad to turn instead to digital hymnals with their rigid, unvarying, programmed tempo. In the office, most likely the first thing we will do (after getting coffee in a disposable cup from a machine) is turn on the computer; this is what signals the start of the day. And when we go to the mall, we select from food packed in plastic, shipped from all over the world. We do not know the people who have grown it and harvested it and prepared it for us. They do not love us – they do not hate us either; we are nothing more than a percentage unit of an annual sales chart. Living this way does not nourish the soul.

But though the IT revolution can make us further isolated, it can also connect us, making new avenues of possibility for otherwise lonely or solitary people. My clothes now are

Whereas nearly three-quarters of people in 1985 reported they had a friend in whom they could confide, only half in 2004 said they could count on such support. The number of people who said they counted a neighbour as a confidant dropped by more than half, from about 19% to about 8%.

General Social Survey of nearly 1,500 Americans, funded by the National Science Foundation, published in the American Sociological Review and reported in the Washington Post by Shankar Vedantam, Jun 23 '06.

On average, in the US, people watch around four hours of television each day. Or one might express this as twenty-eight viewing hours per week, two months of television per year. This means that during the course of a sixty-five-year life, that average American person will have spent nine solid years watching television.

In the UK, the data collected shows similar figures, with some regional variations, showing average daily viewing times ranging from just over three to just over four hours a day.

UK data: Ofcom. US data: Nielsen

Better is a dinner of herbs where love is, than a stalled ox and hatred therewith.

PROVERBS 15:17 KJV

often bought second-hand on ebay, sometimes arriving with a friendly personal note attached or a little bar of soap slipped in as a gift. My son-in-law made his way across the Atlantic to join our family after meeting my daughter online on the Terry Pratchett website! And though television can also be isolating and highly destructive of community, sometimes it makes us aware of lives and people we would never otherwise know, and offers us opportunities for new insights and connections.

Living simply allows us the time and space to think about these things properly, and find a wise and creative balance in the way we live.

I am thankful for the abundance of fruit and vegetables in the street market, the greengrocers and the big stores. The vegetables we grow in our garden at home certainly wouldn't save us in a famine – our success has been mixed and God's bounty has been shared with an army of enthusiastic slugs. But there is something special about it every time we sit down to share a meal that includes the beans and the chard, the tomatoes and courgettes and herbs we have grown for ourselves.

I am grateful, too, for the great machinery of buses and trains: how limited my life would be if I had to travel everywhere on foot! Yet it's important to me in living a discipline of simplicity not to have everything too easy and instant. We do have cars in our family, but they are shared, and many of my journeys are made on public transport. Travelling this way slows you down, no doubt about it: but this is a blessing, not a drawback. Going to a women's meeting in a village a few miles away last spring, I got off the bus to walk the half mile along the road to the chapel. Along the roadside, the banks of earth were clothed with wild herbs and flowers: primroses, dog mercury, celandines. I could have travelled that road every single day and never even known those flowers were there, had I not gone on the bus and then walked. Among them grew drifts of violets, shy and fragrant and utterly beautiful.

Remembering to include the herbs in the bread reminds us of the necessity of beauty for human well-being. Sometimes those who have become convinced practitioners of simplicity, frugality and thrift make the mistake of seeing virtue only in what is cheap and utilitarian. But baking the bread of simplicity is a different endeavour entirely from going to the store to buy the cheapest mass-produced loaf to be found on the shelf. The way of simplicity, like the woman who broke open her jar of spikenard to anoint the feet of Jesus, is in its own way lavish. Gospel simplicity is not miserly or crabbed; it has no vision of scarcity. It celebrates life, it is generous, it creates abundance and freedom; wanting nothing, it is rich.

I go barefoot into the garden to cut herbs. I stop to feel the

To see a World in a Grain
  of Sand
And a Heaven in a Wild
  Flower,
Hold Infinity in the palm
  of your hand
And Eternity in an hour.

William Blake

Voluntary simplicity means going fewer places in one day rather than more, seeing less so I can see more, doing less so I can do more, acquiring less so I can have more.

Wendell Berry

Have nothing in your house that you do not know to be useful, or believe to be beautiful.

William Morris

Be glad of life because it gives you the chance to love and to work and to play and to look up at the stars.

Henry Van Dyke

wind and the sun on my face, to see how the plums are ripening and look for the frogs that hide under the leaves of shady plants near the pond. I stoop to cut a big handful of thyme. It smells just heavenly. As I knead the dough on the kitchen table, the good fragrance is released all through the house.

Choosing simplicity gives us back so much we had lost and forgotten.

Salt

Bread without salt tastes vile. So does porridge. On the other hand, if you put in too much salt, the result is almost inedible. It's vital, but you need only a little.

This is what we can think of as the power of 'small' and the luxury of 'enough'. In the book of Proverbs we discover the wise prayer, 'give me neither poverty nor riches, but give me only my daily bread' (30:8): understanding that surfeit is as destructive as scarcity.

One of the elements we consistently ignore in the teaching of Jesus is what He has to say about smallness and hiddenness. Carried along by the culture of the world that surrounds us, forgetting to be in the world but not of the world, we accept without question the received wisdom that publicity, growth and acclaim are bound to be desirable. When we read the parables of the mustard seed and the sower, when we listen to the reminders that we are to be as yeast in the dough or the salt of the earth, what we have in mind is the big bit, the result: the tree grown from the seed with all the birds nesting in its branches; the hundredfold harvest; the great bread-sponge risen. Forging ahead to the prize, our eyes fixed on the vision of the kingdom we will build – the big building, the great

Let there be work, bread, water and salt for all.

Nelson Mandela

You are the salt of the earth.

MATTHEW 5:13 NIV

A candle light is a protest at midnight. It is a non-conformist. It says to the darkness, 'I beg to differ'.

Samuel Rayan

Whoever can be trusted with very little can also be trusted with much, and whoever is dishonest with very little will also be dishonest with much.

LUKE 16:10 NIV

Go and look towards the sea, he told his servant. And he went up and looked. There is nothing there, he said. Seven times Elijah said, Go back. The seventh time the servant reported, A cloud as small as a man's hand is rising from the sea. So Elijah said, Go and tell Ahab, 'Hitch up your chariot and go down before the rain stops you.'

1 KINGS 18:43-44 NIV

congregation, the people who will make social history – we go galloping right on by the crucial bit of the teaching: that it is by what is small and hidden, so insignificant as to be lost to the eye, that the kingdom begins.

Certainly, in every branch of the Christian family there are those who seem to be called to high-profile public ministry; acclaimed and revered. I have never met them, only heard tell of their fame: but I *have* met, in numbers beyond counting, Christian believers who felt miserable and ashamed because they (thought they) had no public ministry – they became tongue-tied at every opportunity for evangelism; felt appalled at the idea of knocking on the doors of unsuspecting citizens to ask if they knew the Lord; had no account to give of the hope that was in them and, if the truth be admitted, not much hope to give account of.

Well, that's all right: a personality transplant is not necessary. All that's needed is for these believers to start to understand the salt principle.

Jesus said, 'You are the salt of the earth. But if the salt loses its saltiness ['savour' – KJV], how can it be made salty again? It is no longer good for anything' (Matthew 5:13 NIV). That phrase – *salt of the earth* – has passed into our vocabulary to mean people of real solid goodness, of unimpeachable integrity;

and I think that's what Jesus intended it to mean. Salt preserves and cleanses and heals; it cleans wounds and kills bacteria. This should give us a clue to help us understand how Jesus meant us to go about bringing in the kingdom.

Those many believers I have met who felt ashamed and inadequate at their inability to bear witness to the power of the Gospel, have ingested one of the fundamental errors in the thinking of the church; which is that the building of the kingdom comes about principally through the dissemination of doctrine. It does not: it comes about through the transformation of people's lives by the renewal of their minds.

In the task of bringing in the kingdom, regardless of what people may tell you or how it may seem as you look on, I absolutely promise you – it is not how full the stadium was or how magnificent the band; it is not how moving and witty and accomplished the preacher was or the feeling that swept through the crowd; it is not how many 'gave their lives to the Lord' or moaned and wept and promised to follow Jesus. It's all, but all, in the day-by-day quality of the lives they live. And if they can move the crowd and sell their books in thousands; if their name on the advertisement will sell every ticket in the house – even if they heal the sick and raise the dead and speak in tongues and their preaching holds you spellbound until the day breaks: it doesn't matter. Unless the Gospel they preach is what

In spite of everything I still believe that people are really good at heart. I simply can't build up my hopes on a foundation consisting of confusion, misery and death.

Anne Frank

What shall we say the kingdom of God is like, or what parable shall we use to describe it?
It is like a mustard seed, which is the smallest seed you plant in the ground.
Yet when planted, it grows and becomes the largest of all garden plants, with such big branches that the birds of the air can perch in its shade.

MARK 4:30-32 NIV

If your Christianity doesn't work at home, it doesn't work. Don't export it.

Howard Hicks

...be not conformed to this world: but be ye transformed by the renewing of your mind, that ye may prove what is that good, and acceptable, and perfect, will of God.

ROMANS 12:2 KJV

determines their electricity supplier, the car they drive, the way they speak to their families and neighbours and colleagues and the stranger they meet in the street, the toothpaste they buy, the clothes they wear and every minute-by-minute ordinary detail of their lives, they will still hear Christ say, 'Away from me, you evil-doers; I never knew you.'

So often we repeat the error of focusing on getting people's assent to doctrine rather than on seeing their minds and lives renewed starting at the core, the foundation. 'By their fruit ye shall know them.'

The result of this error in thinking leads us, when we think of mission, to think in terms of a special worship programme of events and a publicity campaign, a guest speaker and some exciting attractions: events presenting words of promotion to snag words of assent. Worship, mission, discipleship, evangelism, are thereby degraded to words and events – when we were called to be the salt of the earth.

Salt is a simple, basic thing; but it's tasty. Our calling is to be like that: simple, basic, unproclaimed, hidden, unobtrusive – but tasty and distinctive; there should be nobody quite like us, once the flavour of righteousness has become the determining characteristic of our lives. Nobody eats bread and says, 'Hey, wow! What amazing salt! Taste that salt, man!' If they can taste the salt, you've overdone it. They notice if there's too much or too little: if it's doing its job properly, people don't think about the salt at all; they just enjoy the delicious bread.

Once we have got the transforming power of the Gospel in place in our lives as salt and yeast and light – integral, inextricable, integrated – then the events will become immaterial, because we shall do more evangelism scattered than gathered. Our gatherings then will be entirely for our own mutual encouragement and delight; they won't be campaigns, they will be parties.

'Outreach' will become a thing of the past – we shan't need to reach out because we shall already be there, where the need is and the people are; and we shan't need paid ministers and celebrity speakers because our lives will preach.

What Jesus makes clear is that the seed, the germ, the life-spark of the Gospel – the pilot light that gets the boiler going – is the *hidden* aspect of our lives.

That's the important bit, because it's what generates the future. The hidden aspect, the seed of the Gospel, is the part that's saved. Seeds are saved so that life can always start again. The showy parts – the leaf, the flower – are ephemera; beautiful, necessary, but really in service of the great work of bearing

What do you think? There was a man who had two sons. He went to the first and said, 'Son, go and work today in the vineyard.' 'I will not,' he answered, but later he changed his mind and went.
Then the father went to the other son and said the same thing. He answered, 'I will, sir,' but he did not go. Which of the two did what his father wanted?

MATTHEW 21:28-31 NIV

...be not moved away from the hope of the gospel, which ye have heard, and which was preached to every creature which is under heaven...

COLOSSIANS 1:23 KJV

This is what the kingdom of God is like. A man scatters seed on the ground. Night and day, whether he sleeps or gets up, the seed sprouts and grows, though he does not know how. All by itself the soil produces corn — first the stalk, then the ear, then the full grain in the ear.

MARK 4:26-28 NIV

We know the truth, not only by the reason, but by the heart.

Blaise Pascal

fruit: and the hope lies in the small, hidden life of the seed.

Witnessing to the hope within us according to the salt principle involves:

- Vision

- Perseverance

- Example

- Boundaries

- Restraint

- Explanation

Vision

The power of small, being the salt of the earth and the seed of the Gospel, is about holding the greatness, the magnificence of the Gospel *inside* you. The salt is lost in the dough, dispersed, indistinguishable – but it flavours the whole. The seed is lost in the earth; it is used up as it germinates – in so doing it releases its dream. Here's a small experiment. Take a raw peanut and a pine kernel; you might need a small bag of each, as this isn't totally easy. First with the peanut (because it's easier) and then the pine nut, gently, gently divide them in half lengthwise with your front teeth. In the middle (if you've been really gentle and haven't broken it – if you have, get another and try again) of the peanut you will see the tiniest peanut plant – the dream of the peanut. At the heart of the pine kernel you will find a miniature pine tree – the dream of a forest to come.

In the heart of every convinced Christian lies the dream of the kingdom of heaven; the germ, the seed, the hope of the Gospel. It is released as it is shared and dispersed. The Gospel flourishes when it is released into the wild, not when it is kept contained in steeple-houses and the minister exhorts the already convinced and they use up their energy criticizing each other and raising funds to maintain the building and pay the minister so he can exhort them all over again next week.

Man can't do without God. Just like you're thirsty, you have to drink water. You just can't go without God.

Bob Marley

It is better to light one small candle than to curse the darkness.

Eleanor Roosevelt

As this broken bread was scattered upon the hills, and was gathered together and made one, so let thy Church be gathered together into thy kingdom from the ends of the earth

Didache Apostolorum

You can't be evangelical and associate yourself with Jesus and what he says about the poor and just have no other domestic concerns than tax cuts for wealthy people.

We have got some mountains to move. Three billion people - half of God's children - are living on less than $2 a day.

Jim Wallis

Our true wealth is the good we do in this world. None of us has faith unless we desire for our neighbours what we desire for ourselves.

Mohammed

The magic is that though the dream, germ, spark of the Gospel looks tiny – a buried hope in the heart of insignificant you, inadequate me – it bears the meta-narrative of the salvation of all creation; its potential is colossal.

The way this vision works is integrated and holistic. It starts by beholding and adoring God as creator, sustainer and redeemer, and goes on to unfold and express and expand the implications of who and what God is – right down to the finest detail of daily life. As we let our lives preach, every action and decision becomes a movement of grace.

We wake up in the morning: where are we sleeping? Our bedding will be one of the following:

- Second hand or given to us, so as to save the earth's resources and to be thrifty with our money, so we either have more time or more money to give away.

- Made of organic cotton, because it has been estimated by the World Health Organization that 20,000 cotton workers die each year from contamination, given that about a pound of pesticides and fertilizers will be used to raise the cotton to make a non-organic duvet cover.

- Bought from a fair-trade organization to benefit those struggling to lift themselves out of poverty.

- Bought from a small family firm in our own town, so that we have blessed and enriched the community in which we live, the spirit of enterprise among its people and the freedom to order their lives as appropriate for their circumstances.

- Bought from a trader on ebay, an individual passing on their surplus or operating a modest business from home to augment the family income.

- Got from Freecycle, that wonderful website that exists to keep stuff out of landfill waste sites by putting in touch with each other, with no money changing hands, those who have need of something and those who have something to give.

What our bedding will *not* be is made of non-organic cotton bought at full price from a large chain store that works like a great machine, is concerned only with profit and barrows away those profits from the community from which it derived them, to line the pockets of a few rich shareholders living out their own Mammon dream in some distant place.

That's the beginning of the day.

We stagger out of bed and along to the bathroom to wash. We have made similar choices in our shampoo and toothpaste and

To do evil that good may come of it is for bunglers in politics as well as morals.

William Penn

The Spirit of the Lord is upon me, because he has anointed me to bring good news to the poor. He has sent me to proclaim release to the captives and recovery of sight to the blind, to let the oppressed go free, to proclaim the year of the Lord's favour.

LUKE 14:18-21 NIV

Go and do thou likewise.

LUKE 10:37 KJV

The earth is the Lord's, and everything in it, the world, and all who live in it; for he founded it upon the seas and established it upon the waters.

Who may ascend the hill of the Lord? Who may stand in his holy place?

He who has clean hands and a pure heart, who does not lift up his soul to an idol or swear by what is false.

He will receive blessing from the Lord and vindication from God his Saviour.

PSALM 24:1–5 NIV

moisturisers, sourcing them locally from ethically responsible firms that use a minimum of (recyclable and preferably recycled) packaging, and whose product is created of natural ingredients that are toxic neither to the earth nor the human, and have not been tested in unspeakably cruel experiments on animals imprisoned in laboratory cages.

This way, our lives preach. Before we even get down to breakfast or open our mail, our lives have prayed and proclaimed the Gospel. We have honoured and adored the God who cares when even a sparrow falls, loved our neighbour as ourselves, fulfilled our charge from the Creator to act as His stewards of the earth, remembered the poor and saved our money for the work of the Gospel.

Perseverance

The salt principle is effective and it is what Jesus asks of us, but it is surely not easy to do. For one thing, it takes a lot of thought. In these globalized days, it is extremely difficult to track where all our purchases are sourced. In times when both parents in a family are often employed outside the home, but still the children and household pets must be cared for, the marriage nurtured, the fabric of the house kept clean and in good repair – it seems too much to ask that every purchase, every decision, every choice should be made consciously and prayerfully, a grain of the salt of the earth.

In an era of escalation, high-achieving, multi-tasking, mass-producing, the salt principle is going to be very counter-cultural; so perseverance and determination will be necessary to live this way.

The discipline of simplicity requires us to slow down. We need time to make these decisions, time to think about what we wish to choose and say and do. In fact the apparent achievement of both parents in a family going out to work while simultaneously caring for their household is illusional. We have our time only once, and when it is spent, it is gone. Trying to do too many things equates to doing most things badly. Choosing simplicity gives us the best chance we have of doing the most things well.

It is not the beginning of a matter but the continuing of the same, until it be thoroughly finished, that yieldeth the true glory

Sir Francis Drake

All things come to him who waits.

Proverb

Do not be deceived: God cannot be mocked. A man reaps what he sows. The one who sows to please his sinful nature, from that nature will reap destruction; the one who sows to please the Spirit, from the Spirit will reap eternal life. Let us not become weary in doing good, for at the proper time we will reap a harvest if we do not give up. Therefore, as we have opportunity, let us do good to all people, especially to those who belong to the family of believers.

GALATIANS 6:7-10 NIV

Everything that slows us down and forces patience, everything that sets us back into the slow circles of nature, is a help.

May Sarton

Let me tell you the secret that has led me to my goal: my strength lies solely in my tenacity.

Louis Pasteur

Because it is so counter-cultural, those who choose the way of simplicity must have the tenacity to persevere with very little encouragement – indeed, often in the face of overt and assertive discouragement, even ridicule. Because the salt principle begins in one's own heart and daily life, the first area of witness is one's own household. This is very good for us, because here we are among people who hold the privilege of witnessing in finest detail the authenticity of our commitment to the salt principle – holistic Gospel living, letting our lives preach. The members of our household are the ones who will know if we went straight from the meeting where we were the keynote speaker on compassionate farming to buy a hot (factory-farmed) chicken at the supermarket because we hadn't taken the time to prepare ahead for supper. This means both that the members of our family will be the hardest to convince (and will get the most irritated with us as our daily life presses most nearly upon them) and that once they have been won over, they will be the most comprehensively, unshakeably convinced – and thus will become the source of encouragement and agents of momentum we so need when our own resolve is low.

Until we have at least that core of fellow-travellers, perseverance is crucial to the endeavour. The encouragement for our perseverance must come from the light of the Gospel holding steady in the core of our being; from the voice within our hearts and minds and consciences of the living Christ who has come to teach His people Himself.

Example

The salt principle of building Christ's kingdom on earth is solidly based on example. This makes it slow to begin, because if your example runs counter to the prevailing culture, not only will you set up a social contra-flow that inevitably creates resistance, but onlookers will not recognize (and therefore initially will not understand) what you are doing.

Yet example is the Jesus way of spreading the kingdom. His teaching is shot through with the most scathing condemnation of hypocrisy, and in this emphasis it rests squarely on the foundation of the Old Testament prophets. In every case, the prophetic writings in the scriptures denounce two things: apostasy and social (political) injustice. They advocate, correspondingly, worship that is heartfelt, faithful and true, spilling over into lives of integrity that strengthen community, lift up the orphan, the widow and the alien, make space for the gleaner and remember the poor.

The salt principle creates a framework of social justice, mercy and integrity; starting in the heart and home and working outwards both incidentally and strategically to affect the whole of society. It has innate credibility because of its inbuilt integrity. Teaching without example is no teaching at all.

My life is my message.

Mohandas Gandhi

I said, 'Answer me this one question.' Now keep in mind, I'm planning on witnessing to him. 'If there was a God and he had a church, what would it be like?' He sat there for awhile making up his mind to play or not. Finally he sighed and said, 'Well, if there was a God and he had a church – they would care for the poor, heal the sick, and they wouldn't charge you money to teach you the Book.' I turned around and it was like an explosion in my chest. 'Oh, God.' I just cried, I couldn't help it. I thought, 'Oh Lord, they know. The world knows what it's supposed to be like. The only ones that don't know are the Church.'

John Wimber

What do we do about working with those in need in our communities to help them realise their potential and work towards achieving it, not through fake promises of wealth, but through real and sustainable transformation?

Malcolm Duncan

I am the Lord who heals you.

EXODUS 15:26 NIV

A faithful life generates blessing. A household living faithfully in the way of Gospel simplicity will tend towards stability, prosperity and contentment. Hard times may come – crops fail, banks collapse, natural disasters occur, illness strikes – no one is immune. But the hard times would have come anyway; the household that walks faithfully in the light will be the best equipped to weather the storm when it comes.

There are hard times coming. The lifestyle of consumption and growth we have established is not sustainable. It strips natural resources that cannot be replaced, and uses up those that can, faster than they can be regenerated. It is greedy of land and resources and so tends to incitement of violence and war, and the creation of refugee populations. It pollutes the air and sea and earth, and degrades the land. It creates droughts and floods; and it disempowers and disenfranchises ordinary people even in the rich and powerful countries, let alone in those that are struggling. How could we think hard times would not be coming?

Those who are ready and prepared to take care of themselves and others will be those who know the way of Gospel simplicity. Let me emphasize: *Gospel* simplicity. There is a world of difference between the way of light sustained by prayer and the joy of Christ's presence in the midst, and ways of frugality and abstinence that have no root of spiritual consciousness.

The willingness to set the example of the salt principle involves a ready smile and a spirit of kindness; it is not a way of harsh, unbending, holier-than-thou righteousness. Nonetheless, it implies and requires the setting of firm boundaries.

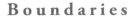

Boundaries

The setting of boundaries when we choose a life defined by simplicity becomes necessary for the reasons set out earlier (in the 'Grain' section): because in a pressured society, anyone who has space and flexibility comes to be seen as a tempting resource to the majority who do not.

But there is a further aspect to the setting of boundaries: it becomes a teaching tool, an aspect of letting our lives preach.

Here is an example. As I was writing the last paragraph, I heard a knock on our front door (which stands open while weather permits) and a voice calling 'Hello.' A neighbour from the next street had come to offer us the wood (for our woodstove winter supplies) from a shed his next-door neighbour was demolishing. He said if we wanted it, he would tell her, and she could just drop the debris over our fence.

I said I would ask my husband when he returned from the barber. The neighbour wanted a quick decision; the woman wanted to know now – could I phone my husband? This seemed reasonable, so I tried his cell-phone; which rang in our kitchen! I said my husband would call round as soon as he returned.

'Oh, I might be out,' came the reply.

> We have freedoms and boundaries; we just have a great family life.
>
> Kelly Preston
>
>

> Good fences make good neighbours.
>
> Proverb

At this point I became conscious of being jerked around. My permission was needed for wood, that my husband might not want, to be fly-tipped into our garden. Our neighbour was relying on the acquisitiveness that infects the whole of our society to pressure me into saying 'yes' if I thought the opportunity might be lost.

So I advised him that if the matter was urgent and the decision could not wait, then his neighbour should make her own arrangements for disposal. Whereupon everything suddenly became less urgent. She could wait to hear, he said. When would my husband be able to let him know?

'As soon as he gets back from the barber,' I reiterated – 'but you're going out.'

'Well, I'll wait,' he replied.

Though it is not boardroom level or the stuff of international mission, this exchange is not insignificant. It involved three households. Refusal to give in to the insistence on everything being done immediately, to the rush and tear which is ruining the whole fabric of our society, to the temptation to grab and get anything and everything on offer, immediately slowed everybody down. They found they had time, after all. That's a kingdom discovery.

Where were you when I laid the earth's foundation? Tell me, if you understand. Who marked off its dimensions? Surely you know! Who stretched a measuring line across it? On what were its footings set, or who laid its cornerstone – while the morning stars sang together and all the angels shouted for joy? Who shut up the sea behind doors when it burst forth from the womb, when I made the clouds its garment and wrapped it in thick darkness, when I fixed limits for it and set its doors and bars in place, when I said, 'This far you may come and no farther; here is where your proud waves halt'? Have you ever given orders to the morning, or shown the dawn its place, that it might take the earth by the edges and shake the wicked out of it?

GOD SETTING
BOUNDARIES!
JOB 38:4-13

It is helpful and encouraging to understand and realise that one of the first spiritiual laws of the universe is that nothing can cross a threshold without permission.

If this is once accepted as true, its implications are immense.

Kelly Preston

Setting boundaries is part of letting our lives preach. My friends who allow their homes to be used for the storage of relatives' overflowing possessions are depriving their relatives of the natural lesson taught by boundaries set and kept. The discomfort of an over-full house, the lack of anywhere to store the accumulated hoard, nudges the householder in the direction of realizing that space and sanity are a matter of personal responsibility, choice and action. It is no kindness to intervene in the lessons taught by reality, by offering an opportunity of avoiding the issue: 'You have too much stuff? Here, store it in my garage.' What kind of a lesson is that?

Restraint

The salt principle is all about the power of small; it involves the consistent exercise of restraint.

In taking the way of simplicity, we learn to recognize that to choose this means to let go of that.

Sometimes I am asked (the tone of voice is usually somewhat bewildered), 'Why did you get rid of that coat/CD player/ candlestick/tea-set etc.? It was beautiful, and you loved it and used it!' The answer is that I wanted the space, the freedom and the flexibility more than I wanted the thing. 'Where your treasure is, there will your heart be also.'

I wanted to be free from the subtle servitudes of paid ministry: my attention was first arrested, then haunted, by the words of one member of a congregation of which I was pastor, reproving me for my refusal to preach on Remembrance Sunday (ever). Explaining that it need not be a difficult thing, or a matter of personal responsibility, she cited the example of the minister who had preached in my stead, saying, 'We told her what we wanted – that's exactly what she did.' I beg God that no one will ever be able to say that of me! My heart's desire is to hear the voice of the Spirit within me, and to be free enough to respond to what *He* tells me to do – not to become a puppet

Restraint and discipline and examples of virtue and justice. These are the things that form the education of the world.

Edmund Burke

Would that there were an award for people who come to understand the concept of enough. Good enough. Successful enough. Thin enough. Rich enough. Socially responsible enough. When you have self-respect, you have enough.

Gail Sheehy

O God, who art the author of peace and lover of concord, in knowledge of whom standeth our eternal life, whose service is perfect freedom . . .

Book of Common Prayer 1928

The Collect for Peace at Morning Prayer

Moderation is the secret of survival.

Manly Hall

I have learned to be content whatever the circumstances. I know what it is to be in need, and I know what it is to have plenty. I have learned the secret of being content in any and every situation, whether well fed or hungry, whether living in plenty or in want. I can do everything through him who gives me strength.

PHILIPPIANS 4:11–13 NIV

with an entire congregation pulling the strings! I have no wish to dominate others or force them to my own point of view; but I will not march to the tune of the band – I hold so precious the freedom Christ has bought me.

I wanted to be free from the necessity of accepting writing, editing and speaking contracts solely to earn money. I wanted to be free to love and cherish my family, my home, my friends and neighbours, and to be flexible to respond if they needed me. I wanted to be free to write the vision God had given me, speaking only when others are listening and when I have something to say.

I realized that the way to purchase this freedom was the exercise of restraint. By simply stopping buying things I (naturally!) reduced my outgoings; but there is still travel and certain essential expenditure to cover. So I sold or gave away almost all my possessions, thus freeing room in our home to accommodate lodgers, whose rent covers the bread-and-butter money – the basic, reliable income. Using a house of good size to accommodate people instead of possessions has to be Good News for the well-being of creation – why heat four spaces when you can heat just one?

So restraint of my own human desires to hoard and accumulate is necessary. I must also restrain myself from straying into scrupulosity. The salt principle is about letting our lives preach by the daily detail of actions and choices: but, overwhelmed as we are by information and opportunity of every kind, it would be so easy to fill my consciousness with a clutter of data and process, until my soul staggered under the burden of all I must remember and take into account to keep my discipline of simplicity squeaky-clean. A rule of thumb that sorts this out is to decide that every purchase or choice must be supported by at least one ethical motivation – so the dress may not be organic or local, but it is fairly traded; the car may use oil to run and pollute the air and require industrial process to produce, but it does have a hybrid engine and it enables us to get to the farm shop; the meal I am sitting down to eat has meat that may have come from a factory farm and vegetables shipped by air from the other side of the world, but it is offered to me in the hospitality of my neighbour's home, as barriers break down and community begins to develop. Ticking all the boxes is not always possible. Restraint is necessary, to avoid fanaticism.

I must exercise restraint in what I ask of myself; harsh and punishing regimes do not build gentle, understanding people. I take tea-breaks; I schedule no more for each day than it is reasonable to expect of myself; I take time to visit with friends and family and enjoy the delight of their company. This may seem normal to you – but I am a bit of a workaholic! At one time in my life I created spreadsheets timetabling every hour of

> I like restraint, if it doesn't go too far.
>
> Mae West

> *Rejoice in the Lord always. I will say it again: Rejoice! Let your gentleness [tolerance, moderation] be evident to all. The Lord is near. Do not be anxious about anything, but in everything, by prayer and petition, with thanksgiving, present your requests to God. And the peace of God, which transcends all understanding, will guard your hearts and your minds in Christ Jesus.*
>
> PHILIPPIANS 4:4–7 NIV

the day, starting at 5.30 a.m., with all the blocks of time filled in, because the day was so crammed that the blocks otherwise blurred into each other. I timetabled sitting-down activities, like preparing liturgies, to coincide with eating my lunch and my supper, so that I could do them both at once. I don't do that any more.

Above all I must exercise restraint in what I say; I must let my life preach, then insert a full stop. If, wherever I go, I must offer a critique on the lifestyle of others, pointing out defects and offering correctives supported by extensive information, I will not be the salt of the earth – I will be an unwelcome bore.

But I still must be willing to give a (brief) account of why I live as I do.

I would add this one reservation: we all need pleasures to keep us going. Remind us of what we ought to be doing, by all means, but remember that moderation itself is only healthy in moderation.

Christopher Manthorp

Never separate the life you live from the words you speak.

Paul Wellstone

Explanation

There is a kind of evangelism that has been described to me as 'question evangelism': your life should be such as to make others ask questions – 'How can you be so patient?' 'Why won't you go with us to see that film?' 'Why do you eat so much vegetarian food?' 'Why do you make your own bread?' 'Why do you give so much money away?' – and so on. When others ask you about your life, you are ready with a brief, gentle, honest answer; bearing witness to the lordship of Christ and the Gospel order by which you create the discipline of everyday living.

If there is nothing about your life to raise any questions, you probably don't need to trouble yourself overmuch about your reluctance to share your Good News with others. Perhaps you need to discover it first for yourself.

First comes the vision; following on from that is the living out of the vision; this is not easy, and will require perseverance as you let your life preach by example. In order to live as an example, boundaries must be set. Restraint must be exercised to maintain gentleness, humour and realism, as well as to remember the larger view, the further goal. And as you persist with this way of living, your life will intrigue the ones who are hungering and thirsting after righteousness; and you must be ready to make explanation of your choices.

Always be prepared to give an answer to everyone who asks you to give the reason for the hope that you have. But do this with gentleness and respect, keeping a clear conscience, so that those who speak maliciously against your good behaviour in Christ may be ashamed of their slander.

PETER 3:15-16 NIV

Let your conversation be always full of grace, seasoned with salt, so that you may know how to answer everyone.

COLOSSIANS 4:6 NIV

The glory of God is a human being fully alive.

Irenaeus of Lyons

The explanation comes at the end of the cycle, but it has the advantage of setting a new cycle in motion: because even as you hear yourself speak, you know there are areas of laziness and neglect and inconsistency; hypocrisies which may have been overlooked by others in their kindness, but which you see all too clearly for yourself.

Living simply gives you time to think, and space to become who you really are. The humour, humility and earthy reality of folk who have chosen to live simply, gives savour and flavour to their words. Their words grow out of their choices and their daily reality: adding the same salt to the mix as their living.

Honey

You have to put sugar in bread, or the yeast won't work.

When Jesus said, 'The kingdom of heaven is like yeast that a woman took and mixed into a large amount of flour until it worked all through the dough', I *know* she put honey in with it; you do have to, to feed the yeast – because yeast is a living organism and sugar is what it likes to eat.

This is a principle of life. Without a little honey in the mix, the lightness won't take off. All of us know dour, heavy, defensive saints; rigid, unbudging, set on being right, harsh and contentious in their manner – and this is not what gets the kingdom built.

So, amid all the discipline and determination, where do we find the honey?

For me, the sweetness of simplicity lies in three areas:
- Freedom
- Relationship
- Self-acceptance

Eat honey, my son, for it is good; honey from the comb is sweet to your taste.

PROVERBS 24:13 NIV

Your food was fine flour, honey and olive oil. You became very beautiful and rose to be a queen.

EZEKIEL 16:13 NIV

'Don't kill us! We have wheat and barley, oil and honey, hidden in a field.'

JEREMIAH 41:8 NIV

Freedom

The freedom of simplicity ramifies into as many areas as it is allowed to touch.

John wore clothing made of camel's hair, with a leather belt around his waist, and he ate locusts and wild honey.

MARK 1:6 NIV

Living in simplicity is about trusting God for each day, and resting in His Spirit, attentive to the quiet guidance that flows lovingly to us in every circumstance of life.

Oftentimes in my work as a minister, people who never normally came to church would brave all the thresholds of an unfamiliar organization to make their way to me with the request: 'Please will you baptize my baby?'

I said to the man who stood at the Gate of the Year, 'Give me a light that I may tread safely into the unknown.' And he replied, 'Go out into the darkness, and put your hand into the Hand of God. That shall be to you better than light, and safer than a known way'.

Minnie Louise Hoskins.

Having told them that yes, God's unconditional love is for everyone, so of course I would baptize their baby, I then went on to ask them: 'But if you never come to church, why do you want me to?'

Most often, the answer was partly about giving thanks for the precious gift of this new life, but partly as a safeguard: 'So that she will be all right'; 'In case anything happens to him'. Perhaps parents who thought along these lines wanted to place their child inside the safety of God's care – even though they weren't quite sure there was really a God, they were willing to err on the side of caution for the sake of their child.

There is a God; and the wings of His protection stretch over us – but people do not always understand what that means. Here is how it works. We come to this world not to pass through unscathed, but to learn how to hold our light steady through every storm and every patch of turbulence. God's grace guides us and keeps us safe, but rather than protecting us *from* adversity, He keeps our souls safe as we pass *through* adversity. Psalm 84 expresses this as: 'How blessed are they who, passing through the dry and bitter valley, manage to find the springs of grace along the way' (my paraphrase). We have to experience adversity, because it will tune and tone our inner being, developing spiritual strength and wisdom. Adversity provides the opportunity for adventures we never expected, and opens the way to riches we never imagined.

The universe is made by God in a particular way, and human beings have a specific place within it. We were made to act justly, to love kindness and compassion, and to walk in humility, close at our Master's side. So long as we do this, the Way will open for us; for we shall be moving forward in the stream of God's grace. There will still be adversity, because that is our teacher, but the Way will be given if we follow the flow of the Spirit in creation. As soon as we try to go a different way, think we know better, want something that is outside God's grace and gift for us, things begin to go wrong. The river of God is powerful and deep, and wading against its current is a bad plan.

He nourished him with honey from the rock, and with oil from the flinty crag...

DEUTERONOMY 32:13 NIV

The ordinances of the Lord are sure and altogether righteous.
They are more precious than gold, than much pure gold; they are sweeter than honey, than honey from the comb.
By them is your servant warned; in keeping them there is great reward.

PSALM 19:9-11 NIV

God whispers to us in our pleasures, speaks to us in our conscience, but shouts in our pains: It is His megaphone to rouse a deaf world.

C.S.Lewis

I call heaven and earth as witnesses against you that I have set before you life and death, blessings and curses. Now choose life, so that you and your children may live and that you may love the Lord your God, listen to his voice, and hold fast to him.

DEUTERONOMY 30 19-20
NIV

Sweet is the work, my God, my King,

To praise Thy Name, give thanks and sing,

To show Thy love by morning light,

And talk of all Thy truth at night.

Isaac Watts

You can see this if you look at the issue of climate change that is so much on everyone's lips. God's intention for humanity was to 'fill and subdue' the earth: that is, to create both abundance and peace. To replenish and calm the earth. To satisfy the earth where it is hungry and parched, and to soothe the earth where it is troubled and wounded. We have not done this. We have been greedy and heedless; snatching heartlessly even from our own kind, let alone God's creatures of other species that we have slaughtered and tortured, for maximum profit, because they got in our way, or even just for fun. We have torn up the earth's treasures without a thought, used up what we call 'resources', forgetting that creation is not all about us. And inevitably, it has backfired on us. Like a stupid man sawing off the branch he is sitting on, we have failed to grasp who will fall hardest in the crash. It is impossible to go against God's command: it just doesn't work. Everything goes pear-shaped when we step outside God's will, because God isn't just a bigger version of a human being but is the source of every kind of truth. God's will is the same as reality; and it makes no sense to think of flouting reality.

To walk in the ways of God we have to learn them, meditate on them, discern them and open our lives to them; and to do this takes a lot of time. Once we have discerned the living way of God, the next step is to align ourselves with it, to walk in it; and that is likely to mean making changes. The changes God asks us to make are often in the direction of being more open and available to our fellow human beings, especially those who are lonely or struggling.

It is simplicity that makes it a viable proposition for us to discern God's way, to make the life changes necessary to walk in His way, and to make ourselves available to love. We won't be able to do this if we are always at work; in the shops; busy with leisure activities; engaged in the upkeep, financing and maintenance of our many possessions – or simply slumped on the couch watching TV.

The way of God not only makes us free, it also requires us to be free: and the key to freedom, as we know, is simplicity.

Agreeing to manage with less is the necessary first step of entering a life of unimaginable abundance.

The freedom of simplicity is one of the sweetest things in my life. Here's an example. At home we have two frightful old cats; ancient, querulous and demanding. Whenever I get up to make a cup of tea, they emerge from the shadows where they lurk, making horrible yowling noises and wanting to be fed. Because they're really old, their body systems are gradually failing. They eat constantly and are often sick. They can't keep their fur free of tangles and hate having it brushed. Despite

God is the friend of silence. See how nature - trees, flowers, grass- grows in silence; see the stars, the moon and the sun, how they move in silence... We need silence to be able to touch souls.

Mother Teresa

If you find honey, eat just enough – too much of it, and you will vomit.

PROVERBS 25:16 NIV

Therefore, as God's chosen people, holy and dearly loved, clothe yourselves with compassion, kindness, humility, gentleness and patience.

COLOSSIANS 3:12 NIV

I expect to pass through life but once. If therefore, there be any kindness I can show, or any good thing I can do to any fellow being, let me do it now, and not defer or neglect it, as I shall not pass this way again.

William Penn

The fruit of the Spirit is love, joy, peace, patience, kindness, goodness, faithfulness, gentleness and self-control.

GALATIONS 5:22 NIV

being ravenously hungry they can't manage any food if it is a bit lumpy or beginning to dry out. They throw up all over the house and what makes it through to the other end is left on the grass in the garden for us to clear up. I inherited one cat with my husband and the other with my house and I didn't want either of them – but the care of them both falls mainly to me.

What I have noticed is that my attitude to the cats depends on how faithfully I walk in the way of simplicity. If I allow myself to take on too many professional obligations, I get harassed and cross – and become impatient with our two furry old ladies. If I spend too much money so that I become worried about the bank balance, anxiety makes me irritable – and then the yowling and endless demands really get on my nerves. If I don't organize my time at home wisely, and am in a hurry – the needs of animals appear absolutely exasperating.

But, if I am spacious and calm, with time in hand and money in the bank, I can see that the two of them are quite sweet really. I look after them properly, and they purr and settle down peacefully, and then I begin to feel successful and magnanimous. It sets up a cycle of blessing.

Living simply allows kindness to expand. It allows tasks to be done well, increases satisfaction and decreases guilt.

Living simply creates time to do things that seemed like forgotten luxuries: read a book; sit by the sea; grow our own vegetables and bake our own cakes; learn to play a musical instrument, or work a lathe, or make our own clothes.

Living simply makes artists and inventors and explorers. One of my daughters, a calligrapher, a ceramicist and a letter-cutter in stone, causes much concern to her grandfather because of her unconventional way of life. Finding her still at home at elevenses time, he brings her cuttings from the local paper advertising jobs to be had at the Child Support Agency. There are always jobs to be had at the Child Support Agency because everyone hates working there. It is a treadmill of the management of other people's misery, hate and aggression. He wants to see her settled in a proper job, with a salary coming in on the last day of the month: but she knows how to live in simplicity – so she has money in the bank while she learns her craft and builds her business; she is content, and if the sun shines she can take time to walk beside the ocean. Which would you rather do?

The freedom simplicity gives us lets us breathe, lets us explore, allows room for contentment. It is honey indeed.

All my possessions for a moment of time.

Queen Elizabeth I

When I work, I work very fast, but preparing to work can take any length of time.

Cy Twombly

I dream a lot. I do more painting when I'm not painting. It's in the subconscious.

Andrew Wyeth

A person needs a little madness, or else they never dare cut the rope and be free.

Nikos Kazantzakis

Relationship

Generally speaking, whether we experience life as sweet or sour depends on the quality of our relationships. That in turn depends on the time, the energy and the level of attention we are able to bring to our relationships. The willingness to walk in the way of simplicity releases time and energy, and enables the quality of attention under which our relationships will flourish.

We are sometimes encouraged to believe that it is all a matter of time management; that it really is possible to hold all the balloons down in the bathwater; and anyway, multi-tasking is cool and we feel superior if we (think we) can cover all the bases.

The best relationships, though, all share a common feature – the element of spontaneity; and the whole point about spontaneity is that it requires you to be available. You can't schedule it, obviously. Magical moments just happen when they do; and the people we grow close to are the ones who just happened to be there to share the magic.

Realizing this, noting an aspect absent from his personal relationships, the busy executive sees the light, schedules in some quality time with the family, twenty-four hours to be

The greatest discovery of my generation is that a human being can alter his life by altering his attitudes of mind.

William James

To put the world right in order, we must first put the nation in order; to put the nation in order, we must first put the family in order; to put the family in order, we must first cultivate our personal life; we must first set our hearts right.

Confucius

spontaneous in; and suffers bitter disillusionment. They have other plans that day; no, thanks, they don't fancy a stroll in the park; sorry, no – they are already going to the cinema with a friend. He schedules an evening to be spontaneous with his wife, and what he plans will spontaneously happen is that they will go out to a quiet little restaurant and then come home and spontaneously make love. Only she wrecks it by not being hungry and falling asleep – the time has gone, it didn't work, and the rest of the week is busy. You can't diarize spontaneity.

Living simply means having time to waste with God and other people; time to dream, time for life to occur, informally, as it does. Living simply isn't something you wedge in, finding a slot for a simplicity moment in the packed schedule of your very successful life. Simplicity is walking an entirely different track.

In the years when I had the privilege of being part of a hospice chaplaincy team, I got used to hearing people make the surprising assertion, in their last month or so on this earth, that this had been the sweetest time of their life; that they wouldn't have missed this for the world. As they took time to explore what they really felt, really believed; sat quietly with those they loved and spoke honestly of that love; allowed others to get close to them, talk about issues that bothered them, comfort them and counsel them gently; as they rested and walked slowly in the garden among the roses – bitterness and anxiety faded,

Don't say you don't have enough time. You have exactly the same number of hours per day that were given to Helen Keller, Pasteur, Michelangelo, Mother Teresa, Leonardo da Vinci, Thomas Jefferson, and Albert Einstein.

H. Jackson Brown Jnr.

There's night and day, brother, both sweet things; sun, moon, and stars, brother, all sweet things; there's likewise a wind on the heath. Life is very sweet, brother...

George Borrow

The culture we have does not make people feel good about themselves. And you have to be strong enough to say if the culture doesn't work, don't buy it.

Tuesdays With Morrie:

Mitch Albom

A house needs a grandma in it.

Louisa May Alcott

'Take teabreaks.'

Bernard Kemp

Beyond a wholesome discipline, be gentle with yourself.

Max Ehrman

Take time to be holy,
Let Him be thy Guide;
And run not before Him,
Whatever betide.
In joy or in sorrow,
Still follow the Lord,
And, looking to Jesus,
Still trust in His Word.

William Longstaff

peace began to establish, life made sense. I am so glad they had that time; but I wish they'd had more than a few weeks of it. I wish they'd known that it can be a way of living as well as a way of dying. Simplicity makes it possible.

When my grandmother's life came to its end, I had three-month-old twins; I was too busy to go and be with her in her last illness. When my dear friend Margery's life came into its twilight, the last months before she died, I was busy getting divorced and struggling frantically to put a workable future in place. When my second husband, Bernard, died, I looked after him to the best of my ability, but kept up my professional commitments – after all, I was soon going to need them. I just about kept the whole show on the road, but I was almost hysterical with exhaustion for much of the time. I hope I have learnt now, that life won't wait until I have some time to spare, to visit its great moments upon me. I have my living to earn: but if I live simply, and my requirements are few, it is possible to guard the freedom that will enable me to respond when the ones God has given me especially to love need me there.

How could life be sweet without relationship? In a crowded, anxious, competitive, speedy, harassed world, simplicity gives my relationships back to me.

Self-acceptance

Simplicity fosters that kind of everyday humility that allows us to accept ourselves. Self-acceptance is a flower of simplicity.

When people feel insecure or not good enough, they may take refuge in status or position, display of wealth, athletic prowess, academic success, or in being one of the beautiful people – chic, elegant, fashionable and thin.

When Gospel simplicity takes a hold on your life, it has the same effect on those concerns as introducing a plough to a manicured lawn. It turns them right over and shows you what's there underneath.

There are some kinds of simplicity – fashionable simplicity, art simplicity, minimalist home design, raw poverty – that may leave illusions and pretensions intact. Gospel simplicity certainly does not.

I am conscious of a little inner hesitation here, knowing that the testimony of my own life might apply less to your life and temperament than I assume. But I feel clear to tell you about it so long as you understand that I am inviting you to look through my window across the valley – I am not hoping for followers or clones!

Do not fear to be eccentric in opinion, for every opinion now accepted was once eccentric.

Bertrand Russell

Therefore, as God's chosen people, holy and dearly loved, clothe yourselves with compassion, kindness, humility, gentleness and patience. Bear with each other and forgive whatever grievances you may have against one another. Forgive as the Lord forgave you. And over all these virtues put on love, which binds them all together in perfect unity. Let the peace of Christ rule in your hearts, since as members of one body you were called to peace. And be thankful. Let the word of Christ dwell in you richly…

COLOSSIANS 3:12–16 NIV

Your life may be the only Bible some people read.

Source unknown

I gave my life to become the person I am right now. Was it worth it?

Richard Bach

The Roots of Violence:
Wealth without work,
Pleasure without conscience,
Knowledge without character,
Commerce without morality,
Science without humanity,
Worship without sacrifice,
Politics without principles.

Mohandas Gandhi

For me, Gospel simplicity breaks down roughly into three areas – Plain living, Plain speech and Plain dress. Though the concept of Plain people is well known in the US, where Amish, Mennonites, Hutterites, Conservative Brethren and Conservative Quakers are relatively plentiful, in England, if I describe a woman as 'plain', I will be understood to be saying she is unattractive. Similarly, in England, 'plain speech' often implies not only directness and lack of pretension, but bluntness to the point of discourtesy.

Even among the Plain people of America, there are differences of opinion as to what does and does not count as 'plain'. So this is my own version, a rule of thumb for my own life, not a requirement (much less a yardstick) to be applied to the life of another.

Plain living, for me, means working with my own hands; continually reviewing (and exercising restraint in) employment of gadgets and machines. To make the bed and hang out the washing in the sunshine, to sweep the floor and weed the garden and wash down the sink, are all part of the creation of order and peace, part of the cherishing of my household, that feeds into the arising of my soul to God in prayer. Keeping firm limits on numbers of possessions, keeping our home clear of clutter and clean from dirt, approaching housework, paperwork and professional duties with method, order and serenity – this to me is the creation of peace and discipline, promoting clear and calm thinking, encouraging mindfulness and recollection.

In some contemplative monastic communities, those newly joining were forbidden for the first year from intellectual labour, working instead in the kitchen and garden, scrubbing the steps, helping on the farm. This helps calm the spirit, shakes pretensions loose, and fosters quietness of mind. It creates the mental space in which any emotional turbulence can make itself apparent and be addressed; physical labour diminishes restlessness and irritability, but it does not allow us to flee from hard questions – on the contrary, it makes way for them to step forward.

Plain living also means owning as little as possible. There's a balance to observe here. Recently we purchased a Wii Fit machine and accompanying TV. I felt nervous about this. Was it just 'one more thing'? But it takes up a whole lot less space than an exercise bike, it's multi-purpose, it fits neatly into the corner of the room, and the money it will save us on gym membership will pay for it in a year – and it's great fun, which is not unimportant. To my surprise, it met my criteria! But, in the kitchen the bread machine is my own two hands, the rice steamer is the same saucepan as cooks the pasta and vegetables, and the soup goes through an old-fashioned mouli-grater.

I tend to limit my possessions by allocating space. I have a

Peace is our gift to each other.

Elie Wiesel

Sometimes people say I should see a therapist, but I don't want any therapist wrecking my weirdness.

Peter Wolf

Take any words in the New Testament and forget everything except pledging yourself to act accordingly. 'My God,' you will say, 'if I do that my whole life will be ruined. How would I ever get on in the world?'

Soren Kierkegaard

Cannot people realise how large an income is thrift?

Cicero

Walk while you have the light, before darkness overtakes you.

JOHN 12:35 NIV

bookcase, three feet six inches by five feet, with four shelves and a little space between the bottom shelf and the floor. When it's full, no more books can come in until some go.

Plain living for me means living with thrift, ingenuity, frugality. To create the freedom necessary to lavish time and attention on my home and family, time spent earning money must be limited. Frugality is challenging and fun; living frugally is a kind of game, full of minor victories and triumphs of the imagination.

And Plain living means restraint in making commitments. I find I can fulfil two areas of commitment satisfactorily; a third overloads things. The two areas I have chosen are family and communicating the Gospel (writing, retreat conducting, helping to prepare other people's writing for publication). It is important to me to take time to visit with my scattered family and be available if they need me, and to create the sort of home where the door stands open, a welcome is offered, and the place is clean, the fire lit and the bread baked when those of us who work out come home in the evening.

Plain speech has not been easy for me. It is about being honest, truthful, direct. It means sometimes not letting things drop but persevering through to an understanding. It sometimes irritates and exasperates powerful people who expected only compliance. You have to be brave, sometimes.

Then again, Plain speech is not confrontational or provocative. It is humble and kind and gentle, considerate of the sensitivities of others. Plain speech means explaining my vulnerability and confessing when I have got something wrong.

Plain speech is wisely leavened with humour; but not so as to evade real encounter or duck out of a difficult issue.

Liking to please people, brought up to seek approval, to 'fit in', Plain speech is difficult for me. I find it hard to state my preferences, hard to be assertive without being aggressive. I make lots of mistakes, but it's very liberating.

Plain dress is about modesty and simplicity in our clothing. This makes a contribution of tremendous importance to our self-acceptance. I went out to supper once with two friends, one of whom is a hairdresser, always smartly dressed and carefully made-up, her hair of course immaculately cut and coiffured. It came out in the course of this conversation that this lady, who was pleasingly plump, expected never – can I repeat that? *Never* – to be comfortable in her clothes. Her fashionable shoes disfigured her feet, made blisters that bled, and hurt her every day. She couldn't possibly have run in them: she must have practised even to be able to walk. Her fitted blouses pulled and her waistband cut into her flesh when she bent down. Her tights were exactly that, and her nail varnish prevented her

The way you speak to others can offer them joy, happiness, self-confidence, hope, trust, and enlightenment. Mindful speaking is a deep practice.

Thich Nhat Hanh

… out of the abundance of the heart the mouth speaketh.

MATTHEW 12:34 KJV

Be still and cool in thine own mind and spirit.

George Fox

Fashion is what you adopt when you don't know who you are.

Quentin Crisp

What a deformed thief this fashion is.

William Shakespeare

Beauty of style and harmony and grace and good rhythm depend on simplicity.

Plato

from doing the garden. She might as well have been trussed up with ropes and tied to the chair!

I feel indignation beyond expression rise up in me when I see what women do to themselves in the endeavour to be sexually attractive. Slimming every day, all their lives, never able to relax their vigilance in the battle to stay thin, they achieve the triumph of an aggressively slimmed body, fed on lettuce and too much protein, and toned by hours on a treadmill in the gym. Of course, though, breast tissue is made up predominantly of fat. Oh dear. Thin women have flat chests and that's not on the list of requirements. Common sense would keep the breasts and stuff the diet. But too many are the women who, determined to make the right sexy product of themselves, choose instead to have surgery, silicone implants swelling their starved bodies, so that they become the toys that men want (or so say the media).

In my own exploration of the ways of simplicity, I have had two or three goes at what dressing Plain might mean for me.

As a young woman, I chose sandals and long skirts – think, basically, 'hippy' – as these were practical, modest and beautiful to me. I liked soft blues and earth reds, moss greens: garments made in India and Afghanistan, coloured with vegetable dyes and still fragrant with the wonderful smell of the East.

A few years ago, beginning to experiment with ways to live that took up the smallest possible amount of space, I tried dressing in saris. Saris are great for simplicity: graceful and feminine, they celebrate the body without loss of modesty or dignity. The layers of a cotton sari are surprisingly warm on a chilly evening, but still cool enough for a hot summer day. I thought I would wear saris forever. They are pretty enough for a party, dignified enough for preaching, ceremonial enough for teaching and conducting retreats, comfortable for everyday, easy to wash and care for, and fold down to the tiniest space for storing. Not only that, but they make groovy net curtains, and fling over the clothes line to make a fabulous chai tent for a party in the garden on a summer afternoon. In my opinion, saris rock.

But I also discovered that saris are political. A Western woman wearing a sari is embracing a culture different from her origins (and while many Asians feel complimented by this, others find it offensive). I realised that wearing saris created incorrect assumptions about my religious and ideological affiliations. I was inadvertently making a statement that was not true about myself. Did this matter? I think, if I had been living in a culture where saris were traditional dress, I should have been delighted to wear them for the rest of my life: but in England where a white woman in a sari is decidedly counter-cultural, I found I was drawing attention to myself; it was no longer possible to slip quiet and unseen through the world. I

If your happiness depends on what somebody else does, I guess you do have a problem.

Richard Bach

Always be a first rate version of yourself instead of a second rate version of someone else.

Judy Garland

Your beauty should not come from outward adornment, such as braided hair and the wearing of gold jewellery and fine clothes. Instead, it should be that of your inner self, the unfading beauty of a gentle and quiet spirit, which is of great worth in God's sight. For this is the way the holy women of the past who put their hope in God used to make themselves beautiful.

1 PETER 3:3-5 NIV

So much has been said and sung of beautiful young girls, why don't somebody wake up to the beauty of old women?

Harriet Beecher Stowe

began to feel my mode of dress sapping my energy – complete strangers stopped me in the street to comment on my clothes; and that did not feel like the way of simplicity. I do still have one or two saris, because I love them – but I keep them for special occasions.

Then, in finding out all that I could about people who choose Gospel simplicity, I felt drawn to the Plain dress adopted by the Amish, the Plain Quakers and the conservative Mennonites. For a little while I dressed as they do, which is beautiful to me – but found that not to be simple in the least! The dresses took up space and needed ironing. Shawls and caps and non-standard underwear were necessary. Nothing was available in stores where I lived – natural fabrics are very expensive, and a lot of fabric went into those dresses. The Plain people asserted that a reason for dressing Plain is to avoid drawing attention to oneself: but that only works within their own communities; dressing like a Plain Quaker in 21st century UK meant people staring at me everywhere I went. I tried to find head-coverings that looked Plain but reasonably normal – but even so my daughter's partner was discreetly and anxiously enquiring of her if I'd had to undergo chemotherapy. I guess if you live in a traditional intentional community in Pennsylvania or Nebraska, Plain dress has a language that makes sense. In my life, it looked like attention-seeking fancy dress. Though modesty has always been important to me, I sensed that, with my hair scraped back tight under a cap and a grey linen loose pinafore dress over a white blouse with a Peter Pan collar, I had moved out of the idiom of my own context.

Back to the drawing board. I was looking for quiet and modest attire, not brash or competitive, flaunting nothing and refraining from using appearance to intimidate others or cause them to feel inadequate. Clothes that would be comfortable, simple to source, hardwearing, easy-care and pack down small to store. I wanted to look feminine, I wanted things that allowed me to feel attractive and confident, but nothing flashy, nothing to draw attention to myself. Part of simplicity, for me, is slipping quietly through the world, going unnoticed through a crowd.

I settled in the end for a selection of cotton jersey tops and comfortable stretchy trousers, with a few skirts (and those saris!) for parties and summer days. I have fleece or linen jackets to keep me warm, and fleece gilets for the winter months. These are all in plain block colours, mostly quiet, neutral shades. Everything tucks into a cardboard box under my bed and twelve inches of hanging space in the wardrobe. On my feet I wear jazz shoes that pack flat, or a pair of trainers if the going is wet and muddy. I wear earrings and a very little makeup – as much as is consistent with travelling light and taking up as little space as possible.

I also want women to dress modestly, with decency and propriety, not with braided hair or gold or pearls or expensive clothes, but with good deeds, appropriate for women who profess to worship God.

1 Timothy 2:9-10 NIV

'Howiver, I'm not denyin' the women are foolish: God Almighty made 'em to match the men.'

George Eliot: Adam Bede

Be humble, for the worst thing in the world is of the same stuff as you; be confident, for the stars are of the same stuff as you.

Nicolai Velimirovic

Setting an example is not the main means of influencing another, it is only the means.

Albert Einstein

I am beginning to learn that it is the sweet, simple things of life which are the real ones after all.

Laura Ingalls Wilder

Just as I am Thou wilt receive,
Wilt welcome, pardon, cleanse, relieve;
Because Thy promise I believe –
O, Lamb of God, I come.

Charlotte Elliott

Uniforms and special clothes create barriers, are separatist and unnecessary. Gospel simplicity has its own kind of Plain; a language of dress that speaks comfortably about humility and natural grace, saying something about what it means for us to feel at home with ourselves.

The 1662 Eucharist of the Church of England's Book of Common Prayer includes a passage of exhortatory scriptures called 'The Comfortable Words'. The Eucharist is celebrated in a more modern idiom these days; but perhaps we might think of our clothing as 'comfortable words', pointing beyond ourselves sacramentally to the Christ and the Gospel that inspire us.

The concepts of Plain living, Plain speech and Plain dress have all contributed to building in me a deep sense of self-acceptance. The Gospel witness of these forms of simplicity also provides me with a wordless daily reminder of my dependency on God: that my life is a web of interwoven grace and trust – 'not by might, not by power, but by my Spirit, says the Lord'.

For me the sweetness of simplicity, the personal reward for the effort and discipline and focus and sometimes self-sacrifice it requires, is the freedom, the space to prioritize the people I love, and the self-acceptance it has brought.

Oil

I have never tried to make bread without oil.

When I worked in a residential care home for children with multiple disabilities, there was a little girl who could not digest fats at all, and she had to be given fat-free bread. Think, 'polystyrene'. It didn't look very nice, though she accepted it patiently.

Staying with my daughters in the summer, I looked at the new packet of bread with the idea (hastily abandoned) of making some toast for breakfast. It was 'slimmers' bread'. Think, 'cotton wool'.

So: bread with very little oil – cotton wool; bread with no oil – polystyrene. Or am I being harsh in my judgments?

When I make bread, I use beautiful extra-virgin olive oil, golden green and fragrant. I put lots in.

When I have kneaded the dough, before I set it to rise, I pour on a little olive oil, and spread it over the whole surface of the lump of dough, to help keep it moist as it rises.

My bread is tasty, and quite chewy – and I think that has something to do with the oil.

Oil in the Bible is for holiness; anointing. It's also for unity. Do you know the Psalm?

> How good and pleasant it is
>> when brothers live together in unity!
> It is like precious oil poured on the head,
>> running down on the beard,
>> running down on Aaron's beard,
>> down upon the collar of his robes.
> It is as if the dew of Hermon
>> were falling on Mount Zion.
>> For there the Lord bestows his blessing,
>> even life forevermore.

Psalm 133 NIV

So unity is precious, blessed, life-giving – and *messy*!

There are many aspects of living simply that require and create order, tidiness and calm. The unity of the people of God is not one of them!

Gospel simplicity is about community. Even if you are living on your own, or nobody you know is interested in simplicity

Thou lovest righteousness, and hatest wickedness: therefore God, thy God, hath anointed thee with the oil of gladness above thy fellows.

PSALM 45:7 KJV

But when you fast, put oil on your head and wash your face, so that it will not be obvious to men that you are fasting, but only to your Father, who is unseen; and your Father, who sees what is done in secret, will reward you.

MATTHEW 6:17-18 NIV

– maybe you even become a figure of fun because of your odd ways – simplicity still affirms and creates community.

The call of the Christian organization CAFOD, to 'Simplicity, Sustainability and Solidarity', makes the connections that help us to understand how living simply always promotes community.

Simplicity is a crucial factor in sustainability – and unless we learn to live sustainably, the climate change that is beginning to make itself felt will escalate into catastrophe. We sometimes are tempted to believe that technological responses will solve the problem – a different fuel, a different machine, a different technique – allowing us to continue to pursue ambitions of ever greater economic growth and development. In reality, the only way forward is to embrace simplicity; to accept, and learn to enjoy, living with less.

An example of this is the vexed question of the relationship between air travel and climate change. Growing awareness of the problems caused by carbon emissions from burning fuel has led to the creation (by airlines and businesses sending executives on international journeys) of facilities, linked to flight bookings, for tree-planting to offset carbon emission. This is a most heartening and encouraging development, a sign of hope: yet there are aspects of environmental change caused by air traffic that these measures do not begin to address.

Forgiveness is the oil of relationships.

Josh McDowell

For our rejoicing is this, the testimony of our conscience, that in simplicity [NIV – 'holiness'] *and godly sincerity, not with fleshly wisdom, but by the grace of God, we have had our conversation in the world, and more abundantly to you-ward.*

2 CORINTHIANS 1:12 KJV

Whether we and our politicians know it or not, Nature is party to all our deals and decisions, and she has more votes, a longer memory, and a sterner sense of justice than we do.

Wendell Berry

Many fertilisers and most pesticides are oil-derived; and most plastics, present in household appliances and office equipment. Textiles for many carpets and clothes use oil based materials. Making a car uses about 20 barrels of oil. Much equipment relies on oil both in its manufacture and to function. Cosmetics, inks, dyes and some medicines depend on oil. The industrial economies would be badly damaged by even a 12% drop in oil production. The real, if not stated, cause of some international aggression and intervention is thought with good reason to be oil. Development in China and India creates fresh demand for oil. Oil was always precious, but we have reached peak oil consumption. Time now to reconsider our options.

The vapour trails ('contrails') that aeroplanes leave in the sky are not only highly polluted, causing air pollution from where they are emitted right the way down to the ground, they are also a form of cloud. Clouds form where other clouds are; so contrails alter the pattern of cloud formation, causing an increase in cloud presence and a related build-up of heat and greenhouse gas. This has not only a slow, long-term effect but short-term and immediate results as well; so much so that a difference is observable between the midweek and the weekend in areas over which heavy air traffic passes.

Changing to bio-fuels (in itself a proposition likely to result in war and tragedy as the poor compete with the rich for crops and land once used for food, now wanted for fuel) does not address the problem, as this requires heavier planes using more fuel and flying lower, resulting in lower contrails and lower banks of cloud, causing increased density of heat and gas build-up.

We can move the pieces of the puzzle around as much as we like: the solution is always the same – *simplify*. Accept less, embrace less; accept that true abundance is found not in accumulation of product but in sharing, in freedom, in relationship, in responsibility; in simplicity.

Simplicity and sustainability are inextricably linked. Living simply, even if not undertaken for that purpose, promotes sustainability; and sustainability implies the adoption of a much simpler lifestyle than is our present norm.

Anything that is not sustainable stops. 'Sustainability' is not just a complicated word beloved of eco-freaks. If our lifestyle does not convert to sustainability then it will stop. It will collapse. Not neatly and quietly, but with hunger, thirst, violence, panic and war. Sustainability is not a minor issue or a hobby; it is the only viable option. Nothing that is not sustainable can continue: and our present lifestyle is not sustainable. If we want to go on living, we have to change. It's not a matter of losing a few beetles in a tropical forest, or even something interesting and furry like tigers. It's everything.

Artists always create in their own likeness. If you look at the work of an artist who paints or draws people, you will notice that those people all tend to have similar faces: that's how you know what the artist's face is like. It is impossible to create anything that is not like you are yourself.

'Hear O Israel,' says Moses to the people of God, 'the Lord your God, the Lord is One.'

The oneness of God is evident in His creation. The word 'universe' itself means 'one song' – the breath of God's Spirit that made all things to belong to one another.

He is the image of the invisible God, the firstborn over all creation.
For by him all things were created: things in heaven and on earth, visible and invisible, whether thrones or powers or rulers or authorities; all things were created by him and for him. He is before all things, and in him all things hold together.
And he is the head of the body, the church; he is the beginning and the firstborn from among the dead, so that in everything he might have the supremacy.
For God was pleased to have all his fulness dwell in him, and through him to reconcile to himself all things, whether things on earth or things in heaven, by making peace through his blood, shed on the cross.

COLOSSIANS 1:15-20 NIV

From the sole of your foot to the top of your head there is no soundness — only wounds and welts and open sores, not cleansed or bandaged or soothed with oil.

ISAIAH 1:6 NIV

So it is that all things are connected; nothing we do remains in isolation. We talk about throwing our rubbish away, but there is no such place as 'away'. The story of Noah's ark brings us this wisdom; it is in understanding that we (all of us, not humans only) are all in the same boat that we will understand God's provision in times of devastation.

What we do to the one interwoven tissue of God's creation, we inevitably do to ourselves.

Simplicity is also integrated with solidarity. As the floods, droughts, tempests and desertification of climate change make themselves felt, with their attendant wars in the scrabble for oil, water and land, the poor suffer worst and suffer first.

They sell the righteous for silver, and the needy for a pair of sandals.
They trample on the heads of the poor as upon the dust of the ground and deny justice to the oppressed.

AMOS 2:6-7 NIV

In twenty-five acres of Borneo rainforest, there can be 700 species of trees. All the rivers of Europe may not contain as many species of fish as one pond in the Amazon rainforest. Indigenous peoples like the Mbuti of Africa, the Kuni of Panama and the Arowaks of Suriname live sustainably in the rainforest. The trees stabilize the climate, protecting the whole area from drought and flood, and supply for the entire world – even people in cities far away – bananas, avocado, grapefruit, guava, heart of palm, mango, passion fruit, papaya, brazil nuts, cashews, macadamia, allspice, cloves, vanilla, black pepper; the list goes on and on.

A quarter of all our medicines already come from the rainforests. Seventy per cent of our anti-cancer drugs come from the rainforest: so do curare to relax muscles for surgery, ipecac for dysentery, quinine for malaria. The rainforest holds the secret of many medicines as yet undiscovered.

And what do we do? We clear-fell the rainforest to raise low-grade beef that can be sold to make hamburgers in fast-food restaurants. *Fifty-five square feet* of rainforest, the home of thousands of species and micro-organisms – more than that, the home of human hope – are lost *for every single one of those hamburgers.* What do you think? Is it worth it?

Food that we call 'cheap' is often cheap in monetary terms alone. In terms of human and animal suffering, loss of bio-diversity, environmental damage, and contributing to violence, poverty and war, it is often very, very expensive indeed.

As we choose fair-trade coffee, tea, chocolate and bananas; as we choose beanburgers over beefburgers; as we check that the wood for our paper, garden furniture, BBQ charcoal, was sustainably grown, we choose life.

Sometimes it costs us more money: so we buy less, but we go on choosing life.

When you reap the harvest of your land, do not reap to the very edges of your field or gather the gleanings of your harvest. Leave them for the poor and the alien. I am the Lord your God.

LEVITICUS 23:22 NIV

Before we can make poverty history, we need to get the history of poverty right. It's not about how much wealthy nations can give so much as how much less they can take.

Vandana Shiva

…the whole creation groaneth and travaileth in pain together…

ROMANS 8:22 KJV

Stop bringing meaningless offerings! Your incense is detestable to me. New Moons, Sabbaths and convocations – I cannot bear your evil assemblies. Your New Moon festivals and your appointed feasts my soul hates. They have become a burden to me; I am weary of bearing them. When you spread out your hands in prayer, I will hide my eyes from you; even if you offer many prayers, I will not listen. Your hands are full of blood; wash and make yourselves clean. Take your evil deeds out of my sight! Stop doing wrong, learn to do right! Seek justice, encourage the oppressed. Defend the cause of the fatherless, plead the case of the widow.

ISAIAH 1:13-17 NIV

The organically raised free-range chicken that allows the bird freedom to roam and does not allow the terrible suffering of deformed and overcrowded broiler birds will cost us more – maybe three or four times more than chicken raised with heartless cruelty and polluting chemicals. So we accept that we can eat it only as a treat, and learn how to cook with lentils, with soya, with delicious vegetables grown in our own gardens and allotments and churchyards.

We cannot see the great trees that our choice to live simply has saved to protect the earth from the ravages of wind and eroded earth; they are far away. We do not see the hens scratching contented in the woodland, laying our eggs for tea. We do not see the child who can go to school, who can be treated at the clinic, because we chose the right kind of tea. They are far away; but they are really there.

Because we lived simply and chose well, took time to think about it and walk the way of God, there is peace and beauty – not only in our own lives but even far away; not only in the lives of children we shall never see, but in the whole fabric of creation, a fabric of which we ourselves are an integral part.

Simplicity and community belong together; even if we live alone. A life lived in Gospel simplicity intercedes every day for the well-being of creation, and the future of all the earth's children.

Simplicity anoints the whole world with the oil of gladness, as Jesus was anointed.

As I mix oil into the dough for my bread, I remember that in the Bible, oil is a sign of holiness.

Holiness is about being in the world but not of the world. Sometimes defined as being set apart for God, holiness implies an awareness of our true nature, a consciousness that we are temples of God's Holy Spirit and bear a responsibility to live in a way that bears witness to His presence.

It is not fitting for the people of God to be greedy and avaricious, acquisitive and gluttonous, stealing from the poor and amassing possessions, investing our hoarded capital in guns and bombs and enterprise we haven't bother to investigate. It is not fitting for us to go into debt acquiring knick-knacks that have called our souls right out of the housing of their proper contemplation into uncontrolled desire for meaningless objects. It brings shame to Jesus when we spend our evenings slouched on the couch in front of the TV, watching graphic portrayals of people torturing each other and blowing each other up, or enjoying as our entertainment actors showing scenes of explicit sexual relationship – often casual, promiscuous and empty of love. We are not walking the way of the Gospel call to love and share and give when we spend £35,000 on a fitted kitchen or

Then the Lord said to Moses, Take the following fine spices: 500 shekels of liquid myrrh, half as much (that is, 250 shekels) of fragrant cinnamon, 250 shekels of fragrant cane, 500 shekels of cassia – all according to the sanctuary shekel – and a hin of olive oil. Make these into a sacred anointing oil, a fragrant blend, the work of a perfumer. It will be the sacred anointing oil.

EXODUS 30:22-25 NIV

But you are a chosen people, a royal priesthood, a holy nation, a people belonging to God, that you may declare the praises of him who called you out of darkness into his wonderful light.

1 PETER 2:9 NIV

A priest happened to be going down the same road, and when he saw the man, he passed by on the other side.
So, too, a Levite, when he came to the place and saw him, passed by on the other side.
But a Samaritan, as he travelled, came where the man was; and when he saw him, he took pity on him. He went to him and bandaged his wounds, pouring on oil and wine. Then he put the man on his own donkey, brought him to an inn and took care of him.

LUKE 10:31-34 NIV

a new car. We have forgotten the image of God in us when we become obsessed with our own image – our status, our position, our sartorial chic. Reeking of whisky and laughing loudly at coarse jokes, we betray the best of what we could have been in favour of something shallow and pointless. We throw away the chocolate and sit chewing the wrapper and wonder why life always tastes so vile.

To live in personal holiness requires a lived decision to step aside from whatever is sinful in our cultural norms: all that is thought racy and exciting and fun; all that is described as 'adult', or 'naughty but nice'.

But at the end of a day spent doing what I like best, writing and caring for my family, when we sit down together with the friends who share our home, to eat broad beans and courgettes and strawberries straight from the garden and herb bread I baked that afternoon – is it likely that I would feel deprived for lack of a day-job, or a ready-meal and a semi-pornographic TV show?

Simplicity is a way that still shines as dusk comes down to night. Simplicity can be hard to choose but it's happy to live.

The way of simplicity heals us. When Jesus healed people from their disease and from possession by evil, He used to describe what had happened as being made whole. Holy, hallowed, whole, healed, holistic – these words all come from the same root. The way of holiness is about being given back to ourselves because we abide in God; it is connected with both integrity and integration. Holiness is about a joined-up vision and a lifestyle free of selfishness and dislocation. Healing and wholeness are inherently holistic; sin isolates, and holiness reconciles.

To live in Gospel simplicity, aware of our connections with the whole human community, protected from loneliness not by an insulating layer of possessions and distractions and machines to play with but by the companionship of those we truly love, is to allow the broken bones of our society to knit together again; allowing all the wounds of separation to heal.

Holiness is love, and love is vulnerable, and vulnerability stands before the beloved in simplicity, bringing nothing to impress but saying only: 'Here I am.'

As for you, the anointing you received from him remains in you, and you do not need anyone to teach you. But as his anointing teaches you about all things and as that anointing is real, not counterfeit – just as it has taught you, remain in him.

1 JOHN 2:27 NIV

Water

In his book *The Hidden Messages In Water*, Masaru Emoto describes his revolutionary experiments demonstrating that water has a memory: it records in its molecular structure intentions of anger... love... fear... kindness... compassion... cruelty.

About 70% of the human body is made up of water.

When I add salt, yeast, honey and herbs into my bread, I just put in 'some'. Approximate amounts will do, creating acceptable variants in the taste. But I always measure the water. In bread, as in all creation, water – but not too much of it – is vital.

Too much water makes a sticky, floppy, unworkable dough – *way* too much and you are out of dough and into batter. Too little gives you a stiff, dry, unworkable dough.

Until you add the water, all you have is a heap of potential ingredients. The moment the water goes in, the alchemy begins.

In his glorious *Canticle of the Sun*, Francis of Assisi describes water as useful and humble and precious and clean. I love it that he identified that quality of 'usefulness' as an attribute of water; for usefulness is a virtue much overlooked. In my childhood among practical Yorkshire people, 'Make yourself useful!' was a crisply spoken injunction often heard. It intrigues and delights me, offering much to ponder on. To tell someone to make herself useful is quite different from assigning to her a particular task: it assumes initiative, expects her to recognize for herself what is needful and supply it. It is community-think, asking that each one assess the work of the group as a whole, identifying and supplying an appropriate contribution to the common task. Just as water is rarely a stand-alone ingredient, but comes mixed with soap to keep us sweet and free from germs, mixed with sugar and salt to save our lives when dysentery racks our bodies, mixed hot with a tea-bag and some milk to help us face everything from the outbreak of war to the start of the 5 a.m. shift; so we as Christians do not stand alone, but offer the vital ingredient of our humble service to the wonderful complexity of the peaceable kingdom, Christ's new order of reconciling love.

It is not possible to overestimate the importance of water on this planet, or the urgency of our learning the lesson of valuing and understanding water, treating the precious and beautiful substance with respect.

In our ignorance, we can make the mistake of thinking the wind to be a random kind of thing: it blows, it doesn't blow; it dries the washing and bends the trees; up a notch and it will lift a barn from one field and deposit it in the next, demolish a house and uproot a mature tree.

If we take time to understand and learn about the wind, we discover that the world's winds – air moving from areas of high pressure to areas of low pressure – follow patterns, and that

About 70% of the Earth's surface is taken up by the oceans.

About 70% of the human body is made up of water.

The salinity (percentage of salt) of the ocean is about 3.5%.

The salinity of human blood... sweat... tears... is about 3.5%

The life of this blue planet is indivisible.

The earth is round.

There is no separation.

What we do to any part of it is ultimately what we do to ourselves.

When Jesus saw him lying there and learned that he had been in this condition for a long time, he asked him, 'Do you want to get well?' 'Sir,' the invalid replied, 'I have no one to help me into the pool when the water is stirred. While I am trying to get in, someone else goes down ahead of me.'

JOHN 5:6-7 NIV

There is the sea, vast and spacious, teeming with creatures beyond number — living things both large and small. There the ships go to and fro, and the leviathan, which you formed to frolic there.

PSALM 104:25-26 NIV

these patterns are determined by water. As the ice-cap melts and freezes with the seasons, so the alteration in temperature determines the patterns of wind and water currents all around the globe. As we continue to build up greenhouse gases, causing the ice-caps permanently to melt, we disturb and ultimately destroy the balance that makes the wind and the water currents.

Without these currents, the world's waters will stagnate. The thermal currents stir the water, and if the waters are not stirred by thermal currents, toxic gases accumulate, eventually to rise and be released. God gave us the treasure of the polar icecaps in the farthest reaches of the north and south, to keep the air and water moving, cleansing and refreshing the whole earth. The polar icecaps were not given as mere challenges to explorers, hostile Nature for daring men to overcome; they watch over our well-being like shining white angels, reflecting away from the earth's surface the excessive heat of the sun. To pollute the earth until we have obliterated the icecaps is to murder the angel of the north, the angel of the south, the watchers in wind and water of the well-being of the world. As the icecaps and permafrost melt, and freshwater overwhelms the saline balance that maintains the thermal cycles of the ocean, simultaneously releasing methane trapped since the last ice-age, as the phytoplanktons die that scrub the carbon dioxide from the atmosphere, the tipping point is reached.

Meanwhile, nearer home, the trees, keepers of water for us all, are felled to make room for concrete developments, for beef ranches, even for the convenience of idle householders who don't like to sweep up leaves. 'That tree's taking over', I hear my neighbours say. Ah. I wish!

In the Gospel story, the man at the Pool of Bethesda sat helplessly, paralysed, unable to benefit from what he knew would save him. When the angel stirred the water, healing came. All he could do was sit and watch as his chances came and went. When Jesus came and found him, he was made whole; released from his paralysis as a passive observer to become a man who could make a difference in the world.

Reading the cold facts of what we have done with our luxury, our pollution, our excess, each trapped in paralysis by the social, political and economic status quo we have corporately created, our chances come and go and we miss every opportunity to be healed. The angel who stirs the water comes, and then is gone, and all we have done is watch it go, and lose the opportunity. May Christ who was with the Father in the mystery of the earth's creating, Christ who in His death on the cross reconciled all things unto God for the healing of all creation, come and find us, and touch us, set us on our feet again and make us whole.

You are this season's people.

There are no other people this season.

If you blow it; it's blown.

Stephen Gaskin

But Zacchaeus stood up and said to the Lord, 'Look, Lord! Here and now I give half of my possessions to the poor, and if I have cheated anybody out of anything, I will pay back four times the amount.'
Jesus said to him, 'Today salvation has come to this house, because this man, too, is a son of Abraham. For the Son of Man came to seek and to save what was lost.'

LUKE 19:8-9 NIV

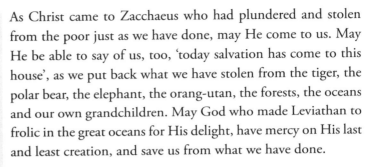

When you throw a stone into a pool, the water responds, but doesn't over-react. The stone makes ripples, then the water is just as it was.
Just as the water reacts appropriately to the stone, then returns to stillness, so the mind that is poised in perfect readiness, resting in God, responds appropriately to life's encounters, returning always to a state of habitual peace. Practitioners of karate call this 'mind like water'. It is the secret of effective living.

As Christ came to Zacchaeus who had plundered and stolen from the poor just as we have done, may He come to us. May He be able to say of us, too, 'today salvation has come to this house', as we put back what we have stolen from the tiger, the polar bear, the elephant, the orang-utan, the forests, the oceans and our own grandchildren. May God who made Leviathan to frolic in the great oceans for His delight, have mercy on His last and least creation, and save us from what we have done.

May God whose voice is in the thunder, who calls the stars and knows the sparrow by name, silence the fatuous prattling of preachers who think Man is the centre of this world that belongs to God. May God heal the waters of this blue planet, and may we find wisdom swift enough to participate in His healing.

In the writings of the ancient Chinese philosopher Lao Tsu, the way of the wise was described as being like water, finding a way round obstacles rather than confronting them, eroding opposition with patience and persistence.

I think Lao Tsu must have been a man who lived beside streams, and meditated on the way of the water-courses. Like Francis of Assisi, he spoke of water as humble, and saw in it the quiet victory of humility: 'the ocean is the king of a hundred streams, because it occupies the lowest place'.

Water is for wisdom teachers the very picture of humility – and humility is one of the richest treasures of Gospel simplicity.

As Christ knelt at the feet of His friends, he brought water to wash away the accumulation of weariness and dust; cool water for the footsore. The way of lowliness – humble, useful, clean and simple – is the way of Christ, the way of water, the way of peace.

Here may I touch and handle things unseen: here grasp with firmer hand the eternal grace, and all my weariness upon Thee lean.

Horatius Bonar

Kneading

Kneading is really important in making bread. You have to knead the dough twice. The first time is the main kneading, which must be done for ten minutes; and the second time, after the bread's first rising, is just a quick, two-minute kneading, often called 'knocking back' the dough before it is shaped into rolls or loaves and set to rise a second time before baking.

I set the timer, when I am doing the first kneading, otherwise I am forever thinking, 'Surely ten minutes has gone by now.' Actually, you can tell when the dough has been kneaded enough, because it takes on a different quality. No longer sticky, it becomes silky and pliable. Even so, having the timer suits my slightly (!) obsessive personality. I like to be sure I have kneaded the bread really thoroughly.

Kneading the dough stretches the gluten, so I'm told. I have no idea what this means, but it's a Good Thing. It is the kneading that makes the dough flexible and gives the bread the correct texture.

When you make pastry, the kneading is done with as quick and light a touch as possible. The pastry dough must be kept cool, and be very little handled. Bread is a whole different

This is the word that came to Jeremiah from the Lord: 'Go down to the potter's house, and there I will give you my message.' So I went down to the potter's house, and I saw him working at the wheel. But the pot he was shaping from the clay was marred in his hands; so the potter formed it into another pot, shaping it as seemed best to him.

JEREMIAH 18:1-4 NIV

animal. The dough is warm because of the living yeast, and the kneading is quite rough and physical. Bread really goes through the mill!

As I accept the call to Gospel simplicity, sometimes it's quite difficult to work out if I'm the person making the bread, or merely the dough itself!

Choosing a way of simplicity involves shaping and kneading and pummelling the stuff of my life, working away at it to get it into the condition that is necessary for it to become the bread of life. As I make mistakes and go back to undo them, or as I get lonely and unsure of myself, I have to keep doggedly on with it, knowing that it will come good under my hands in due course.

The purpose of the kneading is to make the bread both stronger and lighter, and so it is with the work of simplicity.

It is not something that can be accomplished all in a flash. Coming back from a stay with his relatives recently, a friend commented how much he now notices their unmindful habits – wasting food; leaving the TV on standby and the hot tap running; leaving the lights and the cooker on; forgetting to reverence the earth and the Creator by the silent prayer of careful use of resources. Yet only gradually can we be released

No man, having put his hand to the plough, and looking back, is fit for the kingdom of God.

LUKE 9:62 KJV

Therefore if any man be in Christ, he is a new creature: old things are passed away; behold, all things are become new.

2 CORINTHIANS 5:17 KJV

See, today I appoint you over nations and kingdoms to uproot and tear down, to destroy and overthrow, to build and to plant.'

JEREMIAH 1:10 NIV

Damaged people are dangerous. They know they can survive.

Josephine Hart

Yet take thy way;
for sure thy way is best:
Stretch or contract me,
thy poore debter:
This is but tuning of my breast,
To make the musick better.

Whether I flie with angels,
fall with dust,
Thy hands made both,
and I am there:
Thy power and love,
my love and trust
Make one place ev'ry where.

George Herbert

from unthinking patterns into conscious and mindful choice. As we stretch our thinking and imagination and knowledge to reshape our lives, bit by bit a new practice comes about, and new habits are acquired. Time and again I have come home from the high street shops, to sit down with a cup of tea and ask myself, 'Why did I buy that? I don't need it; I don't want it; it isn't ethical. Why did I do it?' And the answer is, I simply forgot. I wasn't paying attention. I let myself be sold an image, an idea. I forgot to keep custody of my eyes and mind, and like a child I let myself be duped and led astray.

I do this all the time – and I have been on this path for thirty-five years. So not surprisingly, when someone comes new to the discipline of simplicity, there seems to be so much to remember and learn, so much of what we are used to and feels comfortable to us turns out to be wrong, that it is easy to be disheartened; being in the world yet not of the world isn't easy.

But we keep working away until the feel of the dough begins to change under our hands. Gradually we feel the silken pliability beginning; we start to feel the benefit of travelling light and remaining flexible, responsive and free. A loved one falls ill, and we are grateful that we left enough spaciousness in our time budget to be able to visit them and care for them. The economy takes a down-turn, and we are so glad that we did not commit ourselves up to the hilt with mortgages and other debts. The sun comes out after many days of rain; and we are glad to have chosen a way of life that enables us to take the time for a walk beside the ocean, in the park, along the canal.

Sometimes, though, I feel more like the dough than the bread-maker! The choice to live simply slaps me around, and I am challenged and confronted by my own shortcomings.

Making more time to think and pray is rewarding and creates peace: but it can be uncomfortable at times, turning into a desert space, a wilderness where I pick up what look like stones and wonder how I ever thought they might be bread.

There is nothing like following a way of simplicity for being brought face to face with my own attachments.

The Gospels are full of clear, strong challenges from Jesus on the necessity for prioritizing the Way of Life and the work of the kingdom above everything else. 'Any of you who does not give up everything he has,' says Jesus, 'cannot be my disciple' (Luke 14:33).

The rest of the New Testament offers no alternative view.

'For me to live is Christ, to die is gain,' says Paul: and, 'What is more, I consider everything a loss compared to the surpassing

> *The tempter came to him and said, If you are the Son of God, tell these stones to become bread.*
> *Jesus answered, It is written: 'Man does not live on bread alone, but on every word that comes from the mouth of God.'*
>
> MATTHEW 4:3-4 NIV

> You must take personal responsibility. You cannot change the circumstances, the seasons, or the wind, but you can change yourself. That is something you have charge of.
>
> Jim Rohn

greatness of knowing Christ Jesus my Lord, for whose sake I have lost all things. I consider them rubbish, that I may gain Christ and be found in him, not having a righteousness of my own that comes from the law, but that which is through faith in Christ – the righteousness that comes from God and is by faith,' we read in Philippians (8:9 NIV).

Who could read and forget the powerful, graphic words of the book of Revelation?

To the church at Laodicea:
I know your deeds, that you are neither cold nor hot. I wish you were either one or the other! So, because you are lukewarm – neither hot nor cold – I am about to spit you out of my mouth. You say, 'I am rich; I have acquired wealth and do not need a thing.' But you do not realize that you are wretched, pitiful, poor, blind and naked (Revelation 3:15–17 NIV).

To the church at Sardis:
I know your deeds; you have a reputation of being alive, but you are dead. Wake up! Strengthen what remains and is about to die, for I have not found your deeds complete in the sight of my God (Revelation 3:1–2 NIV).

And to the church at Ephesus:
I hold this against you: you have forsaken your first love (Revelation 2:4 NIV).

As servants of God we commend ourselves in every way: in great endurance; in troubles, hardships and distresses; in beatings, imprisonments and riots; in hard work, sleepless nights and hunger; in purity, understanding, patience and kindness; in the Holy Spirit and in sincere love; in truthful speech and in the power of God; with weapons of righteousness in the right hand and in the left; through glory and dishonour, bad report and good report; genuine, yet regarded as impostors; known, yet regarded as unknown; dying, and yet we live on; beaten, and yet not killed; sorrowful, yet always rejoicing; poor, yet making many rich; having nothing, and yet possessing everything.

2 CORINTHIANS 6:4-10 NIV

It is not, Christ says, that God does not know we have physical needs, bodies to be warmed and clothed and sheltered and fed; but his challenge is: 'Seek first the kingdom of God and His righteousness, and all these things shall be added unto you' (Matthew 6:33 NIV).

It would be possible to fill this entire book with what the Bible has to say about living lives of radical simplicity, paring away everything but basic necessity (and sometimes even that) so as to be free to walk the way of Christ, free to live with integrity, to worship God and to build the kingdom.

How has it come about that the church has abandoned its dignity and its calling, preferring schism because of a few verses gathered in support of antipathy towards homosexuals, when the great white beautiful shawl of simplicity, the call to live without excess, with no debts, with a minimum of possessions and an optimized, maximized life of freedom and prayer, flung across both testaments, every single book of the Bible, is comprehensively (not even denied) ignored?

When we meet Him, what shall we say? We shall be without excuse, without defence. As usual, we shall have to rely on His mercy.

The great and glorious truths of the scriptures slap my life about like dough on a board, pounding the hell out of it.

We turn to God for help when our foundations are shaking, only to learn that it is God who is shaking them.

Charles C. West

Naked I came from my mother's womb, and naked I will depart.
The Lord gave and the Lord has taken away; may the name of the Lord be praised.

JOB 1:20 NIV

Be it unto me according to Thy word

LUKE 1:38 KJV

Nevertheless, not my will but Thine be done.

LUKE 22:42 KJV

If you break your neck, if you have nothing to eat, if your house is on fire, then you got a problem. Everything else is inconvenience.

Robert Fulghum

Sometimes I feel that it will always be like this, that I will *never* find the equilibrium of this strait and narrow way, *never* achieve the discipline of walking faithfully, my eyes fixed on Jesus.

And then I remember that though this time seems to be going on forever, eventually the gluten is stretched, the dough begins to change texture, the feeling is different, the result looked for at last is achieved.

Simplicity is imperative, and even where it is not chosen, God in His severe kindness visits us with the austere touch of His love in simplicity.

For it is not only from our worldliness and material possessions that God means to shake us free. He will not rest until we are free from every clinging attachment; what we once called idols. Our health; our image; our personal relationships; success; our career; our immaculate homes and gardens; our trophies and achievements; our personal dignity; our doctrine and the addiction to being right.

God knows what we cling to, and one by one He will take out of our hands all these false gods until we are left with only Him.

I fear the road of simplicity, because I have seen all too well where it leads. I have followed in my imagination the Good

Friday road, seen Christ stagger and fall, seen the agony of nails hammered through human flesh, a man hoisted up in the sun to die.

If you're going through hell, keep going.

Winston Churchill

Equally, I have accompanied people dying of motor-neurone disease: seen their distress in being unable to keep from the involuntary moans, unable to get comfortable as neck muscles began to fail, unable to lift the pointer to spell out the words on the board when speech had gone.

I am the Lord, and there is no other.
I form the light and create darkness,
I bring prosperity and create disaster;
I, the Lord, do all these things.

ISAIAH 45:6-7 NIV

I have travelled along the road with the banker, the headmistress, the model, as continence failed and hair fell out and meals were only oatmeal fed from a spoon.

'I will give you treasures of darkness,' says the Lord (Isaiah 45), 'and riches hidden in mystery. I create well-being, I create woe. And I am the Lord who calls you by name. I have borne you this far and I will carry you. Even to old age, I will be enough for you. I am the Lord.'

We cannot truly face life until we face the fact that it will be taken away from us.

Billy Graham

When I consider the road of simplicity that is mapped out for all of us, sometimes my courage fails.

But at least I have enough light to read the story; to know that it is the only way for our souls' health; to grasp that even our extremis is neither abandonment nor disaster, but the darkest blood-red ruby of God's love.

Time

A jug of wine, a loaf of
bread – and thou beside me
singing in the wilderness.

Edward Fitzgerald
The Rubaiyat of Omar Khayyam

*There is a time for
everything, and a season
for every activity under
heaven.*

ECCLESIASTES 3:1 NIV

Most of us love the smell and the flavour of home-made bread. You can even buy a room spray that smells of home-made bread. People who are trying to sell their houses sometimes arrange to have some bread baking to coincide with viewers' appointments, because the wonderful aroma is said to encourage potential buyers to feel they have come home.

Yet though bread-making machines are popular gadgets, very few people make their own bread, by hand, these days.

Kneading dough is an enjoyable, therapeutic occupation. It's not difficult, and it doesn't take long: five minutes to assemble the ingredients, ten minutes for the first kneading, then you're done until the dough is risen. After that, two minutes to knock back the dough and a minute or two to shape it, and you're done until it's risen again and ready to go in the oven. Simple. Easy. Delicious.

Even so, most of us will buy bread ready-made from the shops – and my guess is that this is because the process of making bread is time-consuming. You have to be there. Each stage requires very little input, but you do have to be around and available in readiness for the next stage. Making bread doesn't require complex skills or high intelligence, but it does require attention.

The old Chinese philosopher Lao Tsu said that ruling the universe is like cooking a small fish. He didn't expound on what he meant by this, but the task would be best accomplished by a light and deft touch – you couldn't be heavy-handed with a small fish, or it would come to pieces. Cooking a small fish would be quickly done, but would need constant attention – the cook who wandered off and got distracted would come back to nothing but a small crispy cinder.

Living well, making a success of our finances and our relationships, taking good care of our gardens and our homes, requires a light touch and close, loving attention.

Just as when we bake bread, only a little input is required at each stage, but if we wander off and neglect the process, everything goes wrong, so with our filing of receipts for tax returns, the sowing and watering and harvesting in our gardens, the moments taken to chat and laugh and drink tea together in our marriages, and the fifteen-minute oases of our inner life of prayer. It is the mindfulness we bring, the availability, the remembering to do the right thing at the right time, that creates the good result.

Abraham hastened into the tent unto Sarah, and said, Make ready quickly three measures of fine meal, knead it, and make cakes upon the hearth.

GENESIS 18:6 KJV

A man must be able to cut a knot, for everything cannot be untied; he must know how to disengage what is essential from the detail in which it is enwrapped, for everything cannot be equally considered; in a word, he must be able to simplify his duties, his business and his life.

Henri Frederic Amiel

Time is the coin of your life. It is the only coin you have, and only you can determine how it will be spent. Be careful lest you let other people spend it for you.

Carl Sandberg

To laugh often and much; to win the respect of intelligent people and the affection of children... to leave the world a better place... to know even one life has breathed easier because you have lived. This is to have succeeded.

Ralph Waldo Emerson

The apostles gathered round Jesus and reported to him all they had done and taught.
Then, because so many people were coming and going that they did not even have a chance to eat, he said to them, Come with me by yourselves to a quiet place and get some rest.

MARK 6:31 NIV

When my children were small, in the school holidays, I knew that they did not need a relentless programme of activities and scheduled recreation. They liked to spend hours in the garden making mud pies and make-believe. They liked to play in the rock-pools at the seashore. Too much adult intervention was unhelpful and discouraged independence: but they needed to know I was there to turn to. I learned as a mother that being available is an activity in itself. It was no good my getting absorbed in an occupation of my own that could not be left – the times when I was writing books and could not be interrupted generated considerable stress!

On a normal day, I used to take up my station in the corner of the sofa, occupied with some task of no immense importance, while the children hummed about on their own vital business. I remember watching my twins go by, at about eighteen months of age, dressed like refugees from *Little House On the Prairie* (pretty dresses are easier to come by second-hand than track-suits), purposeful and intent, each with a baby doll held firmly in one arm and an old spoon clutched in the other hand, off to make unspeakable stews from slugs and earth and flower petals.

They didn't want my intervention, they wanted to be free. But when someone fell and grazed a knee, their return heralded by the roars of agony and misery increasing in volume as they came back down the garden, they expected to find me ready with a plaster and some ointment, some arnica and a kiss, when they burst in wailing through the kitchen door.

And when the urge to do some drawing or colouring came upon them, they needed me there to turn to: 'Mummy – draw me a mermaid… draw me a princess…'

Sometimes a moment of private conversation was necessary to clarify a small confusion: 'Mummy, is that insect in the garden called a grasshopper or a tennis?' ('I think you may be thinking of a 'cricket', Grace; is it brown or green?')

What a store of precious memories I would have lost, had I never been available. That treasury of sweet memory would have become the property of a childminder.

When my husband Bernard was dying, many nurses came and went, many people upheld us in prayer, many friends telephoned and sent cards, and I was so grateful for all their love and care. But best of all were my daughters, who in the last few weeks said, 'We've come to stay': not to do anything in particular, just to be with us; and Bernard's dear friend Mike, who would come by with a reading book, and just sit in silence at Bernard's bedside reading, companionable.

The Lord is my shepherd, I shall not be in want. He makes me lie down in green pastures, he leads me beside quiet waters, he restores my soul. He guides me in paths of righteousness for his name's sake. Even though I walk through the valley of the shadow of death, I will fear no evil, for you are with me; your rod and your staff, they comfort me.

PSALM 23:1-4 NIV

For where your treasure is, there your heart will be also.

MATTHEW 6:21 NIV

There are no words to express the abyss between isolation and having one ally.

It may be conceded to the mathematician that four is twice two. But two is not twice one; two is two thousand times one.

G.K.Chesterton

The day before Bernard died, Mike's daughter got married, and the family were caught up in a whirl of celebrations. But Mike came by even so, with some wedding food for us who were watching, and to spend half an hour sitting with Bernard as he always did. Then, needing to go back to his family, he got to his feet, bent over Bernard and left one light kiss on his brow, saying, 'Goodbye, old friend,' before leaving.

The Disney cartoon film, *Wall-e*, imagines a time when human beings leave the task of cleaning up the earth, made uninhabitable by mountains of trash, to a machine called Wall-e. Sorting through the piles of rubbish, crushing what is worthless and storing what is re-usable, Wall-e comes upon a diamond ring still in its presentation box. Uncomprehending, he saves the box and throws away the jewel.

And how often have human beings done the selfsame thing? Kept the mortgage, the salary, the image, the television, the car, the hobby – and thrown away the time to walk together by the river, to watch the sunset, to notice the baby frogs climbing in the grass in early summer, to make a lonely elderly relative glad with a visit, to go to church, to go outside on a frosty night and look up at the stars.

These things I am describing seem so small – of so little consequence that they are often brushed aside.

In the years when I worked as a Methodist pastor, considering a new appointment that meant a move away to a new location, I voiced something that was troubling me: 'What about Margery?' Margery, dear friend and prayer partner, old, going blind, relied on me so much. The man of whom I asked the question, a successful businessman, shook his head. 'Forget Margery,' he said, going on to explain to me that in the 'real world' it is more important to focus on earning a living and making a shrewd career move – friends, family, the children, the old, the lonely: these must be left behind, not allowed to get in the way of achievement.

I took his advice, and I wish I had not.

Love the Lord your God with all your heart and with all your soul and with all your mind and with all your strength.
Love your neighbour as yourself.' There is no commandment greater than these.

MARK 12:30-31 NIV

Fire

If you make meringues, you have to cook them so slow and cool they are more drying than cooking. If you make a baked custard you place the dish inside a container of water to slow things down, and cook it gently so it doesn't curdle. If you cook cakes, the oven is taken up to a moderate heat; and the bigger the cake, the cooler the oven, so that the top doesn't begin to burn while the centre is still half-raw.

But bread has to be cooked in a hot oven. Such a simple, robust food, it asks for no special cosseting and can be even more delicious cooked in a clay oven out of doors.

The bread of simplicity also needs to cook hot. Simplicity is a dreary business without fire.

There is the simplicity of the poor, which can be a miserable, anxious existence spent wondering how to fend off creditors, and working long hours of drudgery just to survive. There is the simplicity of those who are merely indifferent: who don't care what they eat or what they wear or what they do, and live lives unruffled by the stirring of ambition or aspiration. There is the simplicity of the very rich, who pay others to do the work that would otherwise take up time, who enjoy a life free of clutter because everything and everyone else is just disposable.

Gospel simplicity is not like that.

Like a child with a magnifying glass focusing the sun's light onto a little heap of dry leaves and twigs until it smoulders and kindles into flame, Gospel simplicity single-mindedly focuses the fire of the Holy Spirit onto the ordinary things of daily life until they are alight.

Gospel simplicity is a matter of passion and focus, our time on this earth lived with what athletes call a 'quiet eye' – the ability to maintain steady focus throughout the turbulence of activity required of them.

The discipline of simplicity is the magnifying glass that focuses the sun, so that the concentrated force of the Holy Spirit can be trained upon the insignificant bits and pieces of the common way in which we tread, effecting amid all the dross and distractions the living fire of a kindled life.

The practice of simplicity is the quiet eye that focuses the athlete's attention, so that our own forces of attention are gathered in orientation upon one single goal – the opening of ourselves free of clutter, division or distraction, so that the kingdom may come on earth as it is in heaven.

The way of simplicity, then, is like Jacob's ladder: a column

He will baptize you with the Holy Spirit and with fire. His winnowing fork is in his hand, and he will clear his threshing floor, gathering his wheat into the barn and burning up the chaff with unquenchable fire.

MATTHEW 3:11-12 NIV

The biggest thing [Frida] brought into my life was this peacefulness. I still get passionate about things, but my passion is not so scattered and it's not needy. It's a lot more powerful because it comes with this groundedness and peacefulness. That it's about the process, not about the results.

Salma Hayek

of unshadowed light raised between earth and heaven, which allows both for the ascent of our intention and the descent of divine empowerment. Simplicity purifies, refines, quietens and distils, until the living ray of our relationship with God illuminates the entire landscape of our lives.

The wonder of simplicity is its double action, which creates a self-renewal once it becomes a habit. For simplicity both requires vision, the fire of God's Spirit, in order that life be inspired rather than merely deprived, and at the same time sets the conditions for the inspiration it requires. Living in simplicity allows a soul to feel the need of God, to ask the big questions, and to experience the existential weathers and rhythms, the ontological forces that drive our being. As we take away the toys and the hobbies, the treadmills and the frantic pressures, the preoccupation with image, and status and expectation, the great questions arise. What does it mean, to be a human being? What am I here for? Where is God in the midst of suffering and grief? What does it mean to live in a world where some are scratching a living for their children on refuse heaps while others are lonely and insecure in mansions and yachts under the relentless searching eye of the paparazzi? How is it possible to balance the benefits of scientific (especially medical and agricultural) and technological advance with the natural imperatives of the eco-system to affirm and enhance the well-being of *all* creation? How might we hear with respect

> Don't ask yourself what the world needs; ask yourself what makes you come alive. And then go and do that. Because what the world needs is people who have come alive.
>
> Harold Whitman

> While women weep, as they do now, I'll fight; while children go hungry, as they do now I'll fight; while men go to prison, in and out, in and out, as they do now, I'll fight; while there is a drunkard left, while there is a poor lost girl upon the streets, while there remains one dark soul without the light of God, I'll fight – I'll fight to the very end!
>
> William Booth

and empathy the many voices of a culturally and theologically diverse world while at the same time bearing with integrity the unsullied light of Gospel truth?

We have no time for these questions as we are fending off emails and driving down the slipstream into the eighty-mile-an-hour traffic on the motorway. Have you ever seen film footage of stockbrokers on the floor of the stock exchange in the fever of business? Do you think their minds and souls are held in quiet focus upon God?

I heard a modern young mum describing a breakfast encounter in her home. Her elderly father's birthday was upon them, and she was unprepared, with no card or gift – certainly no time to visit. She persuaded her four-year-old son to draw him a picture, to restore the sense that someone in the family cared. The child drew while she scurried around doing all that must be accomplished before she could leave the house and take the children to nursery, then continue to her important work as a civil servant. Multi-tasking seemed to have triumphed: but then the child asked that Mother in her turn draw a picture for him. Pressured by the many tasks to be done, she refused. The child insisted. To make the point that her boundaries were set, and because she had no time anyway, she still refused. The child had only one weapon left – retaliation: 'Then I won't choose *you* to read my story!' he said.

Speak softly, people will listen: take your time, the world will wait.

Source unknown

A hundred years from now it will not matter what my bank account was, the sort of house I lived in, or the kind of car I drove... but the world may be different because I was important in the life of a child.

Forest E. Witcraft

Marriage is under pressure, both from the emptiness of fragmenting society and from the restlessness of the human heart.

Elaine Storkey

Then one of the seraphs flew to me with a live coal in his hand, which he had taken with tongs from the altar.

With it he touched my mouth and said, See, this has touched your lips; your guilt is taken away and your sin atoned for. Then I heard the voice of the Lord saying, Whom shall I send? And who will go for us? And I said, Here am I. Send me!

ISAIAH 6:5-8 NIV

The young mother, in telling the tale, expressed her pride in her child – he had learned the power of negotiation. I saw it differently. My heart broke for him, as I heard what she had to recount; for it seemed to me that he had learned a terrible lesson – in a society where the people have no time for one another, abandonment is the normal revenge.

When Christian people are asking themselves what it is that God is calling them to do in this life, I believe there is one thing they can take for granted: it is God who gave them their children, and God intends that they should occupy themselves with loving and caring for those children until they are of an age to take care of themselves.

For a mother to stay home and care for her children, cook for her family, make the home welcoming and clean and kind, in these days when the price of accommodation assumes both partners in a couple to have a full-time wage, can be accomplished only with the skills and resourcefulness of committed simplicity. It needs the sustained fire of determination and conviction to carry it through: that these precious young lives are more important than luxuries and holidays and wine on the table and meals in a restaurant and new clothes every season, and the kudos of professional success. That this vocation, to be a mother, is worth all the borrowing from Peter to pay Paul, and living on carrot-and-lentil stew and waiting until the reduced food in the supermarket is reduced again twenty minutes before closing time; and bread and tap-water is good enough, and broken biscuits on days when there is no money for bread, if that is what it takes to raise your own children, yourself.

Simplicity is a fiery thing.

In the days when our five children were still very young, a sophisticated friend commented on our lifestyle choice of simplicity: 'I envy you your gentle walk,' he remarked to their father, who gazed at him speechless. 'He has no idea,' he said to me later; 'he has not the first idea what it costs.'

To live simply costs everything; but it gives you everything in return.

Simplicity allows me to touch the blessing of God's refiner's fire. In diminishing the heap of my personal possessions, there have been times when to part from some treasured item felt like a surgical operation. I could feel the hold it had on my soul, and to give it away uprooted something very deep. Yet as soon as it was selected for disposal and put out ready for the charity shop, its magic vanished – it became nothing more than the worthless item it really was; useful or not useful, but nothing more than that.

A family is a place where principles are hammered and honed on the anvil of everyday living.

Charles Swindoll

Is not my word like fire,' declares the Lord, 'and like a hammer that breaks a rock in pieces?

JEREMIAH 23:29 NIV

Most people are other people. Their thoughts are someone else's opinions, their lives a mimicry, their passions a quotation.

Oscar Wilde

Quiet minds can't be perplexed or frightened, but go on in fortune or misfortune at their own private pace, like a clock during a thunderstorm.

Robert Louis Stevenson

Do not let your fire go out, spark by irreplaceable spark, in the hopeless swamps of the approximate, the not-quite, the not-yet, the not-at-all. Do not let the hero in your soul perish, in lonely frustration for the life you deserved, but have never been able to reach. Check your road and the nature of your battle. The world you desired can be won, it exists, it is real, it is possible, it's yours.

Ayn Rand

The more possessions I parted company with, the more precious felt the freedom I had won, the time to spend with my family, to wonder, to think, to pray, to preach and teach and learn. As life became more spacious, a new thing began to happen: I started to notice how flawed is my character, and experience my faults and inadequacies. I think God must have been drawing these things to my attention, because this didn't feel demoralizing or depressing – just illuminating, interesting and instructive. It became a new aspect of the discipline of simplicity, freeing me from compulsions and prejudices, from poses I had adopted and ideas I was attached to. The modern preoccupation with money to be made from copyright has created the concept of 'intellectual property'. As my life became more spacious I had the opportunity to notice that I had acquired rather a lot of 'intellectual property' – intellectual baggage, in fact; intellectual clutter.

Dropping it in the intellectual disposal bin as I prayed and thought, I found myself freed of certain stances and persona; I discovered myself to be not a particularly nice person, and this came as a surprise, for I had had always prized the sense of myself as someone of great integrity.

The gap between what I am and what I ought to be became so obviously wide as I looked more deeply, and my hunger for simplicity so intensified, that I resigned from ordained ministry in the church, desiring to strip back my life to the bedrock, to nothing but the essentials of being alive in Christ and answerable to His Spirit. This step brought a new freedom; for ordained status is wrapped in a dense tissue of expectations, preconceptions, power, and the need to pretend. I became free to know a clearer honesty, and to be silent when I had nothing to say, instead of being propelled to the front to 'say a few words' on every possible occasion.

Chipping away at the ossified accretions of a lifetime, I see the figure of Christ beginning to emerge: and Christ looks different from me. I notice my irrationality, my obstinacy, my fearfulness and tendency to bear grudges, now that His face is coming clearer: but though I feel ashamed that these are part of me, I am not alarmed about it. If I continue in the way of simplicity, the spaciousness will allow His light to sluice through and through me; and in time I know His light will wash me clean.

A friend once told me of discovering in the back streets of Jerusalem a man refining gold, in a pot over a fire. As he heated the pot, the dross (like the scum you get when you cook pulses, I suppose) would rise to the top, and he would skim it away. Patiently, repeatedly, he skimmed away the dross, and my friend asked him when he would be satisfied – how he would know when the gold was finally ready. The man said he would

You taught me to be nice, so nice that now I am so full of niceness, I have no sense of right and wrong, no outrage, no passion.

Garrison Keillor

The Lord make his face shine upon thee, and be gracious unto thee: the Lord lift up his countenance upon thee, and give thee peace.

NUMBERS 6:25-26 KJV

know the gold was ready when he could see in it the reflection of his face.

Shew me a penny. Whose image and superscription hath it? They answered and said, Caesar's. And he said unto them, Render therefore unto Caesar the things which be Caesar's, and unto God the things which be God's.

LUKE 20:24-25 KJV

God bends over this world, skimming away from our lives the useless accumulations of trinkets and gadgets, of status and intrigue, of legalism, sophistry – all the accretions and complications that cloud our simplicity.

He is looking for the people He made in His own image: Adam and Eve – 'Earthy' and 'Life'. When He can find them again, when the dross is finally skimmed away so that their lives are open to the blessing of the light of His countenance watching over them, then life on earth will be able to flow as it should. As things are at present, all we seem capable of is producing more and more dross – more wars, more corruption, more selfish divisions. How hot will God have to make His refiner's fire before we give up all that sullies and corrupts us, and offer Him lives of such simplicity that He may once more behold, in what we are, His face?

I don't want to know about evil;

I only want to know about love.

John Martyn

Some of the adversities and challenges we put down to 'enemy attack', thinking them to be satanic because they disrupt our lives and create blocks and obstacles, are I think in fact the refining fire of God; uncomfortable heat applied to change and refine us. Climate change, the soaring cost of living and accommodation, stress, depression and burn-out –

so widespread now in our society – and many other ills, are opportunities to reconsider, to cut back to a manageable scale, to attempt less and achieve more.

In his wonderful and valuable classic book, *Pain, the Gift Nobody Wants* (Paul Brand with Philip Yancey), Paul Brand examines the role of pain in human living, classifying it not as an enemy to be overcome, but as a friend whose warnings are given to guide and help us. What is true in the case of the individual human body is also true in the case of human communities, of the planet that is our home – wherever there is pain or disease or dysfunction, there are lessons to be learned.

So often, it is the pressure of life hurtling along at a hectic pace, driven by the imperative of financial borrowing, that prevents us from giving the necessary attention to converting adversity to wisdom. Advertisements encourage us to ignore and silence pain. When we are overstretched by impossible demands in the workplace, the pharmaceutical companies have a solution: not simpler lifestyle but stronger and stronger painkillers for our headaches, our gut-aches, our soul-aches.

Living simply allows many such aches and ailments to subside naturally. Those that persist, we have time to address thoroughly and understand properly, once we stop running long enough to look and think.

Praise be to the God and Father of our Lord Jesus Christ! In his great mercy he has given us new birth into a living hope through the resurrection of Jesus Christ from the dead, and into an inheritance that can never perish, spoil or fade – kept in heaven for you who through faith are shielded by God's power until the coming of the salvation that is ready to be revealed in the last time. In this you greatly rejoice, though now for a little while you may have had to suffer grief in all kinds of trials. These have come so that your faith – of greater worth than gold, which perishes even though refined by fire – may be proved genuine and may result in praise, glory and honour when Jesus Christ is revealed.

1 PETER 1:3-7 NIV

This is all that I have learnt: God made us plain and simple, but we have made ourselves very complicated.

ECCLESIASTES 7:29 GOOD
NEWS BIBLE

I believe the single most significant decision I can make on a day-to-day basis is my choice of attitude. It is more important than my past, my education, my bankroll, my successes or failures, fame or pain, what other people think of me or say about me, my circumstances, or my position. Attitude keeps me going or cripples my progress. It alone fuels my fire or assaults my hope. When my attitudes are right, there is no barrier too high, no valley too deep, no dream too extreme, no challenge too great for me.

Charles Swindoll

If we try to justify our journey then we are lost.

Jackie Pullinger

The refiner's fire of God, who is our friend, is not only a matter of moral purification, but is about a process of attaining simplicity for our own well-being, for the good of human society and all creation.

Not all suffering and adversity is the heat of God's refiner's fire encouraging us to change. Sometimes we are called to suffer for others, or to act courageously so that change may come, or to bear the consequences of wrong choices made by other people. Even when that is so, simplicity is our friend.

When he was called to fight the giant Goliath, David was given Saul's armour to wear. Unused to battle-gear, and too slight in stature to fit the mail made for someone else, David found it nothing but an encumbrance. He went out to do battle with the giant armed with no more than his sling and some pebbles from the brook: and it was enough.

When we are called to face giants of adversity, huge and daunting challenges, we stand a better chance of emerging victorious if we are not encumbered and weighed down. We cope with the challenges that are ours to face more effectively when we are not hampered and cluttered by complications and distractions of our own making.

To live simply has its own fieriness: it is an exacting discipline requiring character and perseverance: but to choose simplicity is to step out of the Saul's armour that would have hampered us at every turn; the 'benefits' that become a dead weight in the field. To live simply is to step into your own being, free, and open your soul to God's undiluted reality.

Waste no more time talking about great souls and how they should be. Become one yourself!

Marcus Aurelius Antonius

Blessing

When I have made bread rolls, and I hold them in my hands still warm from the oven, and break them, I touch something of the life of Jesus.

The best of it is, God is with us.

John Wesley

He stood in the desert looking at the stones that reminded him of bread. Some of my 100 per cent wholewheat rolls might remind Him of those stones!

He took bread in his hands and blessed it, and broke it; all these centuries later, here I am doing the same.

Whoever possesses God in their being, has him in a divine manner, and he shines out to them in all things; for them all things taste of God and in all things it is God's image that they see.

Meister Eckhart

Jesus blessed the bread by giving thanks. This has very big implications for the way I can live my life in the ordinary everyday.

I believe that blessing effects change; it makes a difference. To say to someone 'God bless you', to consciously speak a blessing, is to release Holy Spirit power into their life.

Jesus taught His disciples, when they went to stay in someone's home, to say 'Peace be to this house.' He said that if a man of peace is there, their blessing of peace would rest on him: if not, it would return to them (Luke 10:5–6).

So there is a two-way dynamic in blessing: the one who sends forth power in words of blessing, and the life that opens itself to blessing by flowing in the same direction as the intention of the words.

The example of Jesus, blessing the bread by giving thanks, teaches us that gratitude sanctifies our life and makes it happy. This two-way dynamic means that we can both open our lives to blessing, to holiness, by practising an attitude of gratitude; and we can power blessing into life by saying 'thank you'.

These two aspects of blessing might be seen as word and deed. It is our actions, the way we live every day, which open our lives to the power of the blessing when it is spoken.

Gratitude is expressed in what we say – 'thank you!' – and how we live; treasuring God's gifts of life, relationship, the wonder and beauty of the living earth, clear water to drink, a home to live in, warm clothes to wear, a bed to sleep in, something to look forward to for supper.

If someone gives us a gift and we ignore it, trash it, tread on it, destroy it – that would not count as gratitude. It would not be possible to bless a recipient who had such an attitude. When we spoke the words of blessing, they would find no 'man of peace' to settle on, and would simply return to us again.

Throw your bread out onto the waves: you will see, in the end it will come back to you.

ECCLESIASTES 11:1
(PARAPHRASE)

In our daily lives, we must see that it is not happiness that makes us grateful, but the gratefulness that makes us happy.

Albert Clarke

My imperfections and failures are as much a blessing from God as my successes and my talents and I lay them both at his feet.

Mohandas Gandhi

Infinite growth of material consumption in a finite world is an impossibility.

E.F. Schumacher

Whatever befalls the earth befalls the sons of the earth. Man did not weave the web of life, he is merely a strand in it. Whatever he does to the web, he does to himself.

Chief Seattle's Testimony

Every man is a missionary, now and forever, for good or for evil, whether he intends or designs it or not. He may be a blot radiating his dark influence outward to the very circumference of society, or he may be a blessing spreading benediction over the length and breadth of the world. But a blank he cannot be: there are no moral blanks; there are no neutral characters.

Thomas Chalmers

This is the situation we are in with regard to the earth our home, today. Though in church on a Sunday we may sing hymns that praise God for creation or pray in the intercessions for peace and the well-being of creation, human actions rarely create the conditions on which those blessings may settle. When there are flash-floods and droughts, wars over land use, violent storms, then we pray to God to lift the curse of these terrifying phenomena and still the storm with His word. Our prayers release blessing which hovers over the earth, looking for a life of peace upon which to settle. Not finding one, they just come back to us again, like Noah's dove. For our prayers and blessings to go all the way, to be effective when we send them into the world, we have to have created the right conditions for them to settle upon: we have to be living what we pray for.

In the book of Genesis, when God makes human beings and names them, His choice of name suggests His intention for them.

'Adam' is a play on words, derived from the Hebrew word for 'earth' (*adamah*). 'Eve' means 'life'. What a wonderful blessing these two names invoke, acting in harmony together in dominion over the earth. Adam will recognize that the earth is what he comes from, what he is made of, what he is called to care for; and Eve will choose life, bring forth life, act to protect and nourish and nurture life.

If we truly desire to be biblical people, living lives of blessing empowered by the Holy Spirit, we might think about stepping into the power of our naming. We are sons of Adam, daughters of Eve; together made by God to bless the living earth. Creation groans, is racked, is hanging on by a thread, waiting for the sons of Adam and the daughters of Eve to wake up and know who they are, see what power to bless lies within them, turn away from selfishness and open their lives as a beautiful channel of blessing. God waits for us so to enter simplicity that we are no longer full of ourselves, no longer so dammed and clogged with our own greed for power and possession. God waits for us to become clear again.

In His parable of the sower, Jesus speaks about the seed of the Gospel that falls among thorns. He says that these represent the cares and pleasures of this world, which will rise up and choke the life out of the Gospel as it tries to grow and mature in our lives. It's not always easy for us to understand that it is the pleasures as much as the cares that can choke the Gospel, and it can be puzzling to discern which cares and pleasures are the worldly sort that will clog up our souls, and which are the legitimate variety that will make us wiser and enrich our souls.

A friend of mine went through a tough time with his family: his marriage was unhappy, one of his children was very sick, life was hard. To cheer himself up and please his wife and as

> The ultimate test of a moral society is the kind of world that it leaves to its children.
>
> Dietrich Bonhoeffer
>
>

> The purest expression of the Christian faith is essentially dissident. The nearer it comes to being an 'establishment' religion, the further it is from Christ and the fainter his voice becomes, a voice which calls his followers into inevitable conflict with the status quo.
>
> Murray Watts
>
>

> The Christian's chief occupational hazards are depression and discouragement.
>
> John Stott
>
>

I have three things I'd like to say today. First, while you were sleeping last night, 30,000 kids died of starvation or diseases related to malnutrition. Second, most of you don't give a shit. What's worse is that you're more upset with the fact that I said shit than the fact that 30,000 kids died last night.

Tony Campolo

The salvation of one's own soul, or self-sanctification, or self-perfection, or self-fulfilment may well be the goal of Buddhism or Greek philosophy or modern psychology. But it is not the goal of Christianity.

Vincent Donovan

a distraction from his anxieties about his child, my friend bought new living-room furniture from a shop that ran a 'buy now, pay next year' scheme. This brought a flicker of false happiness, followed by a very large debt to add to the problems he already had.

Seeking refuge in material possessions solves nothing. Even though human nature is tempted into quick fixes to provide temporary relief from drawn-out times of hardship and sorrow, the wisest course of action is always to stay close to simplicity. Living simply helps us to discern what is good for us.

My dear friend Margery lived a very disciplined life. She loved the Lord, and consulted Him in prayer about every day and every decision. She lived frugally, wasting nothing. By national average income standards, she was quite poor, but always thought of herself as rich, because she always had money left over. Because she was so unpretentious, people trusted her, and often told her their troubles. She gave generously to charities, but she especially loved to help those who were just ordinary folk struggling – people not eligible for charitable grants or government support, but finding it hard to make ends meet. Seeing their trouble, she would ask the Lord, 'Should I help?' If He said 'Yes', she would ask Him, 'How much should I give them?' She would wait for the whisper of His voice in her soul, and give exactly as much as He told her to. This quiet, thoughtful sharing of what little she had blessed so many people. It left her with a very small income indeed; but she still thought she was rich, because her needs were so simple that she always created a surplus. She lived on about half the income of some of my friends who were quite sure they were poor.

Simplicity blesses. It is as easy as that. It blesses our own lives and every life that touches ours.

One of the things I keep learning is that the secret of being happy is doing things for other people.

Dick Gregory

Breaking

When I was at ordination school, we had a delightful, funny, kind, loving tutor called Alan. In the retreat house where we stayed for some of our tuitional weekends, they baked the most delicious bread rolls every morning. One day as we sat at breakfast, my friend Paul (not really thinking about what he was doing because he was engrossed in a conversation about the resurrection) was trying to tear his roll in half, to butter it. The bread was substantial and chewy, just as it should be, and did not come apart very readily. Alan, amused, was watching Paul's absent-minded efforts. 'You're going to have to do better than that when you're ordained!' he joked – which brought us back to present reality and made us laugh.

But bread does break relatively readily. Compared with substances like rubber or bamboo, bread is easy to break.

To dismember someone is to tear their body apart. When we remember, we recall them, make them whole again, for a moment bring back into reality the person we have lost.

So the Eucharist offers the wisdom that gathering and scattering, dismembering and remembering, are part of the rhythm of joy and sorrow, finding and losing, wounding and healing, being

When you reap the harvest of your land, do not reap to the very edges of your field or gather the gleanings of your harvest. Do not go over your vineyard a second time or pick up the grapes that have fallen. Leave them for the poor and the alien. I am the Lord your God.

LEVITICUS 19:9 NIV

Even if I knew that tomorrow the world would go to pieces, I would still plant my apple tree.

Martin Luther

A broken and contrite heart, O God, you will not despise.

PSALM 51:17 NIV

born and dying and rising again, the heartbeat of human living that makes us what we are.

The *Didache*, one of the earliest writings of the Christian church, says of the Eucharist: 'As this broken bread was scattered over the hills and then, when gathered became one mass, so may thy church be gathered from the ends of the earth into Thy Kingdom.'

In the breaking of the bread, we remember Jesus on the night in which He was betrayed, knowing what lay before Him, ripping the bread apart in His hands, saying, 'This is my body...'

We tear the bread to pieces, dividing it out among us; but this is where the mystery begins. For as we share it and eat it, what was torn apart, broken and divided, draws us together in one. We receive the bread saying, 'Though we are many, we are one body because we all share in the one bread.'

As we remember Him, Christ is no longer broken, His life scattered and spilt, but found in living presence in our midst as we draw together in one circle of shared life.

Human life and happiness, like bread, offers little resistance to the forces that tear it apart. It is not hard to break bread, and it is not hard to break a person, a family, a marriage, or a human community.

What will you answer? 'We all dwell together to make money from each other'? or 'This is a community'?

T. S. Eliot, Choruses from *The Rock*

Love a man, even in his sin, for that love is a likeness of the divine love, and is the summit of love on earth.

Fyodor Dostoyevsky

Faith is the strength by which a shattered world shall emerge into the light.

Helen Keller

Time is a great teacher, but unfortunately it kills all its pupils.

Louis Hector Berlioz

The desert is squeezed in the tube-train next to you.

The desert is in the heart of your brother.

TS Eliot (Choruses from The Rock)

The simplification of life is one of the steps to inner peace. A persistent simplification will create an inner and outer well-being that places harmony in one's life.

Peace Pilgrim

A bruised reed he will not break, and a smouldering wick he will not snuff out.

ISAIAH 42:3 NIV

Those of us who make up twenty-first-century society have witnessed or experienced wars and genocides of unbelievable cruelty. We have seen urban life with its isolation and anonymity spawn violence, gun and knife crime and property crime. Consumer lifestyle has brought freedoms that have liberated some lives but ruined others. As women became financially independent, family life has begun to crumble – for in marriages where love has died, only need holds people together. Mass production of material goods has created ever more complex and sophisticated requirements in daily living; personal affluence has become the cuckoo in the nest as workers covet more and more money to keep up with payments on homes and belongings they expect and are expected to own, but cannot really afford. Jealousy and anxiety, weariness and a sense of inadequacy, turn people against one another as economic pressures squeeze individual lives relentlessly. Personal relationships turn sour and community networks loosen and unravel, integrity is compromised and kindness evaporates, as economic imperatives tighten their grip until they become the norm that defines our setting of priorities.

'This is my body!' cries Jesus, as he rips the bread apart in His hands. We might well say the same of human community everywhere, as we watch and listen to the international news.

The church that Christ prayed would be one body, would be

completely one as He and the Father are one, has not been immune to schism and alienation.

The holy scriptures under whose authority we unite also offer the bone of contention over which we divide. With every new division, those who leave blame not their own faithlessness but the weakness and corruption of those who stay.

'This is my body!' Crumbs thrown out for the birds.

Yet as we receive the Word into our hearts and lives, and we gather and share, as we confess our sins and tell the story, share the kiss of peace and eat together in simplicity, humility and thanksgiving, we discern the body again.

As we lay down the affluence and accumulation of possessions; the arrogant attachment to being right, the obstinate clinging to our own way in all circumstances, a resurrection begins to happen, we discover that we need each other, and community can flower again.

When Jesus warned us that only if we became as a little child would we obtain the vision of the kingdom of heaven, it was a call to simplicity.

We are asked to leave our stubborn insistence on our own

Everyone thinks of changing the world, but no one thinks of changing himself.

Leo Tolstoy

'When do we get to do the stuff?

John Wimber

(on living what we read in the Bible)

No act of kindness, no matter how small, is ever wasted.

Aesop

The violets in the mountains have broken the rocks.

Tennessee Williams

We who lived in concentration camps can remember the men who walked through the huts comforting others, giving away their last piece of bread. They may have been few in number, but they offer sufficient proof that everything can be taken from a man but one thing: the last of the human freedoms – to choose one's attitude in any given set of circumstances, to choose one's own way.

Viktor Frankl

perspective. We are asked to see only how vulnerable we are, and how lonely life can be. We are asked to realize as a child does that life is terrifying on your own, that we each need someone to look after us.

When Jesus said, 'This is my body', what He held in His hands was not a fat packet of title deeds, or a catechism laden with footnotes, or a breviary so thick it overbalances on the lectern, or a Bible commentary that explains with triumph why all those who disagree are wrong – He held in His hands only bread, torn for everyone to have some.

'This is my body'; bread for the life of the world, uniting not divisive, sustaining, accessible.

Bread breaks so very easily; but in its brokenness it unites around one table all the people who are willing to share, transforming them into the *laos*, the household of faith – one family.

'Faith' is a multi-layered word, compressing into its smallness so many shades and nuances of meaning.

It has to do with personal experience and also with tradition. It holds a resonance about loyalty and deep abiding; constancy. It implies a life that looks upward and reaches beyond itself. It involves exploration of mystery, but reaching that in the ordinary tasks of work and home and family. It expresses commitment.

The exact mix of what 'faith' means is bound to be unique to each one of us; your emphasis and vocation will not be exactly like mine. Yet I think there are three aspects of faith that will always be part of its manifestation: faith will always be about relationship, faith will always live overshone by a greater light, and faith will always feed upon the bread of simplicity.

By this means, looking beyond ourselves to the others who share the circle with us, and beyond the circle to the God who is our light, what started as a breaking, a dis-membering, can be re-membered as a sharing that draws us together into one circle of simplicity.

Sharing is the essence and life of simplicity.

My own reasons for choosing to live simply are:

- Unless we live simply we will destroy this earth, causing immense suffering in the process (war, disease, famine, toxicity).

- If I live simply my life becomes freer, happier and more spacious: I have more choices and my money goes further.

'Gather up the fragments that remain, that nothing may be lost.'
JOHN 6:12 KJV

When you remember me, it means that you have carried something of who I am with you, that I have left some mark of who I am on who you are. It means that you can summon me back to your mind even though countless years and miles may stand between us. It means that if we meet again, you will know me. It means that even after I die, you can still see my face and hear my voice and speak to me in your heart.

Frederick Buechner

'Jesus, remember me
when you come into your
kingdom'.

LUKE 23:42 NIV

'Never ask, 'Oh, why were
things so much better in
the old days?' It's not an
intelligent question.
Everyone who lives ought
to be wise; it is as good as
receiving an inheritance,
and will give you as much
security as money can.
Wisdom keeps you safe –
this is the advantage of
knowledge.

ECCLESIASTES 7:10-12
GNB

- Living simply strengthens my spirit, allows me to see Jesus more clearly, and allows me to listen to the still, small voice of God.

- Living simply makes me more accessible as a human being: more available and less intimidating.

To live in simplicity and fulfil these aspirations, I have to accept the discipline of owning and consuming less. Techno-wizardry will not provide solutions in every case. For example, those who share my concern about climate change and the well-being of eco-systems recognized the need to reduce carbon emissions. When the reality of peak oil began to be understood, alternatives were sought. Bio-fuels were welcomed as the great new solution: if we used palm oil, everything would be okay. Only a few metres down that road, it dawned on us we were heading towards nightmare. To run machinery on bio-fuel on a massive scale would hugely exacerbate the conflict that already exists over the human race's use of land. Agricultural land and crops would be taken from the poor to produce fuel for the rich. The precious remains of the rainforest would be clear-felled for palm-oil production. This solution is no solution: it's just a worse problem than the one we had before.

There never will be solutions that do not involve consuming and producing less.

The key to reducing consumption without simultaneously reducing quality of life lies in sharing.

Sharing resources – living space, transport, possessions and daily life – addresses at a stroke many of the ills of our society: depression; isolation; the increased cost of living; loneliness; vulnerability (perceived or real) to attack, theft and burglary; selfishness and the refusal to be accountable; wastefulness; clutter; pollution – sharing is the way to deal with all these things. The only thing that stops us sharing more than we do is the dread of not being able to have our own way all the time.

When Jesus broke the bread at the last supper, saying, 'This is my body', he used the neuter form of the Greek word 'this', which cannot agree with the masculine *artos* (bread). The 'this' of which Jesus was speaking was not the bread only; it was the breaking and the sharing of the meal.

We are fooling ourselves when we try to reduce what Jesus said and did to religious ritual. How could Christ have possibly meant that we would re-member Him, that He would be there in our midst, if we went through certain ritualistic actions involving certain ritualistic elements? What can that possibly have to do with the Christ we read about in the Gospels?

We become the body of Christ when we allow ourselves to be

Confront the difficult while it is still easy; accomplish the great task by a series of small acts.

Lao Tsu
(tr. Stephen Mitchell)

Kindness has converted more sinners than zeal, eloquence or learning.

Frederick W. Faber

The miracle is this – the more we share, the more we have.

Leonard Nimoy

broken as easily as bread; and when we are willing to share, making sure that everyone is included, and nobody left out.

We are not the body of Christ at all if we snatch and grab for ourselves and leave the poor hungry and dispossessed, thrown off their ancestral land so we could have it for beefburgers. We are not the body of Christ when we drive through the world in fuel-hungry utility vehicles, guzzling our children's future for a selfish status symbol today.

Two disciples made their way from Jerusalem to Emmaus in much the same state of mind as many of us experience today: bewildered, grieved, unsure what to do for the best.

Jesus walked with them, and explained the scriptures to them, and their hearts burned within them. But their eyes were opened, new vision and hope returned, when they invited Him in to share their supper, and He took the bread in His hands and broke it…

In similar wise today, the scriptures can do little more than give us spiritual heartburn until we pick up the ordinary stuff of our daily lives, and (with thanksgiving) break it and share it out. Then we will begin to see Christ in the midst of our community. Then it all begins to make sense.

There must be more to life than having everything!

Maurice Sendak

It is only the heart that can really see. The essential is invisible to the eye.

Antoine de Saint Exupéry

How wonderful it is that nobody need wait a single moment before starting to improve the world.

Anne Frank

Enjoying

A brief moment from a TV interview has stayed in my mind over decades. A glamorous, slim, blonde, beautiful young TV presenter was given the task of interviewing an elderly monk about his daily life. Brimming with vitality, her eyes flashing seductively, she quizzed him about his favourite food, probing for confessions of forbidden luxuries. He thought carefully, then told her quietly and seriously that his favourite food was brown bread.

It was not, I think, the interaction that the producers had been hoping for; but it was a moment full of truth.

With real wisdom, the monk had identified that in the end it is the ordinary that sustains us – not the special, the unusual, the luxurious, the exotic.

One of the difficulties inherent in modern life is its tendency to rob us of the ordinary.

Striving for the complete kit of home, furniture, motor vehicles, electronic gadgetry, career opportunities, leisure pursuits (with associated paraphernalia), clothes and accessories, beauty treatments, gym membership, processed food, fine wines,

You have to live every day as if it's your last, because one of these days you're bound to be right.

Breaker Morant

It's human nature to get distracted by minor issues. We play Trivial Pursuit with our lives. Henry David Thoreau observed that people live lives of 'quiet desperation,' but today a better description is aimless distraction. Many people are like gyroscopes spinning around at a frantic pace but never going anywhere.

Rick Warren

holidays, and all the etceteras, we offer up, in exchange, life's most precious gift to us: our time.

In the liturgical cycle of the church in which I was raised, the bulk of the Sundays were numbered according to their proximity to Trinity Sunday. A change made during the years I was serving as an ordained minister renamed these Sundays as the 1st, 2nd, 3rd etc., in Ordinary Time. I found this change delightful, and felt so grateful to have ordinary time celebrated for so much of the liturgical year. Ordinary means of course both 'unexceptional' and 'ordained'. 'Ordinary' has its own technical resonances in liturgical vocabulary, but it was not that but the elevation of ordinariness *in the ordinary sense* that delighted me. The brown bread of life, the Plain food that sustains us when the fancy morsels lose their appeal.

Ordinary time is the treasure of our lives, and however many toys we get in return for it, we are always the poorer for its loss.

Living simply allows us to keep the ordinary time God gave us, to use as the light within us best determines.

When the time came that I judged my children old enough for me to work outside the home, I was surprised by an economic phenomenon I later discovered many others have rumbled by now: the second income of a household is swallowed up in

He who dies with the most toys wins.

Bumper sticker

When Alexander saw the breadth of his domain, he wept for there were no more worlds to conquer.

Plutarch

Everybody, soon or late, sits down to a banquet of consequences.

Robert Louis Stevenson

One of the universal rules of happiness is: always be wary of any helpful item that weighs less than its operating manual.

Terry Pratchett

solving the problems created in its generation. Ready meals for a whole family, because no one was home to cook, prove expensive. Buying a second car to facilitate the management of childcare and travel to a second job is expensive. Special outings, clubs and treats, to compensate children for not being able to come home and having no parent available to play with them, take a big bite out of income. Special clothes for work cost money. Childcare is very expensive. The second income generated by both parents going to work is almost entirely absorbed in compensating for the loss of the homemaker: and there is no one home to clean, cook, do the laundry, take in deliveries, care for the animals, the elderly, the sick and distressed, look after the children, or offer a welcome.

Living simply and frugally, making one income stretch, is a form of blessing.

Two of the greatest and most enjoyable blessings of simplicity are the return, to modern people, of their own time and their homemakers.

Another wonderful blessing of simplicity is choice. Those who live simply, with very few possessions, in small dwellings, with modest needs, making their own entertainment and amusement, have far more flexibility and more real choice. This is true even if they are poor, because such an approach to life can mean the

> I've learned that people will forget what you said, people will forget what you did, but people will never forget how you made them feel.
>
> Maya Angelou

> A good rule of thumb is if you've made it to thirty-five and your job still requires you to wear a name tag, you've made a serious vocational error.
>
> Dennis Miller

Reduce the complexity
of life by eliminating the
needless wants of life, and
the labours of life reduce
themselves.

Edwin Teale

When you take time to ask
yourself what you came
here to do, remember
to include that you have
been entrusted with the
privilege of making those
close to you feel special and
appreciated.

He who buys what he
does not need steals from
himself.

Source unknown

difference between being poor and getting by, and getting into a downward spiral of debt. When a whole church community is living simply, sharing their homes, income and possessions, then church members can be kept out of poverty to enjoy a better and happier quality of life.

I vividly remember the point at which, in my children's growing years, their father's income reached the point where it was possible for us to have ice-cream in our freezer and soda in the fridge on a regular basis, whereas previously these had been treats reserved for birthdays. At first I was delighted. Then it dawned on me that the main outcome of this change was that the whole family had lost its treats. Treats now would have to be something bigger and better than ice-cream and soda. Increasing affluence removes from us, one by one, all our treats.

I am a firm believer in treats. In my ordination school we had one summer a visit from a guest lecturer who had been chaplain to the (then very elderly, now deceased) Queen Mother. He told us that every morning this disciplined and doughty lady asked of her ladies-in-waiting what duties her diary held for that day. And having taken in the duties of the day, she next asked: 'And what treats are we having today?'

This is wisdom! Life has to have treats, or we lose hope and good courage. One of the many blessings of simplicity is that it allows us to keep all our treats.

Living simply also greatly enriches and blesses the imagination. Those of my family who share my delight in living simply can spend hours planning imaginary lifestyles based on simplicity: possible layouts for multiple-occupancy homes involving the construction of private alcoves and ingenious fitments; the management of heat, cold, personal hygiene and sleeping arrangements for travellers taking to the road on foot with only a rucksack to carry. This is not flippancy, the insular middle class who know nothing of how the poor live: sometimes in the road we have travelled we have found ourselves without a proper home, with no idea how to finance our continued existence – the game of living simply has been both our practical necessity and our entertainment. Singing folk-songs while toasting marshmallows over a fire of saved-up junk mail, cardboard packaging and fir-cones collected from the road-side, is not a hardship – it's fun! Shaking out a big bag of cast-off clothes from a friend's rich sister in the big city is not pitiable – it's exciting! Waiting for parcels in the post after bagging a bargain on ebay is much more fun than the concrete foot-slog of the high street.

Years ago when Ron Sider wrote *Rich Christians in an Age of Hunger,* he was sharply criticized for challenging his readers

From time to time, we need to remind ourselves to relax, to be peaceful, we may wish to set aside some time for retreat, a day of mindfulness, when we can walk slowly, drink tea with a friend and enjoy being together as if we were the happiest people on earth.

Thich Nhat Hanh

Straightforwardness and simplicity are in keeping with goodness. The things that are essential are acquired with little bother; it is the luxuries that call for toil and effort. To want simply what is enough nowadays suggests to people primitiveness and squalor.

Seneca

Consider the lilies of the field, how they grow; they toil not, neither do they spin: and yet I say unto you, That even Solomon in all his glory was not arrayed like one of these. Wherefore, if God so clothe the grass of the field, which to day is, and to morrow is cast into the oven, shall he not much more clothe you, O ye of little faith?

MATTHEW 6:28-30 KJV

to give up some of their consumer habits. His suggestion that they probably now had enough pairs of shoes and need not buy another pair over the next year or two created consternation – struggling shoemakers everywhere would be out of business!

When we live simply, though, stepping aside from the rat-race of consumerism, nobody loses but the fat cats of the big corporations. Living simply allows us the choice to buy (when we need it) a pair of shoes from a shoemaker, instead of cheap, shoddy shoes made in an overseas sweat-shop and sold in a chain-store to line the pockets of its shareholders. If we live simply enough, we probably have the time to learn how to make our own shoes. If the shoemaker is living simply too, he doesn't need to sell so many shoes anyway; so maybe he will be able to reduce his overheads by working from home, which will enable him to reduce his childcare costs and make his own bread. Living simply is not utopian pie in the sky; it's practical, it works, and it blesses everyone.

Yet of all the blessings of simplicity, the one that has surprised me most is the sense of well-being – of sheer happiness and light-heartedness – it has brought me.

Until I began this adventure, I had not understood that consumerism (which is slavery to Mammon) is an addiction. Maybe a heroin addict needing a fix feels that what would really make him happy is more heroin, when actually the greater happiness would be the freedom from the addiction. In the same way ordinary householders, who do not perceive themselves as addicted, think they need the new winter coat in the shop window, the moisturiser advertised in the women's magazine, the car that will make them look like James Bond, the promotion that will cover the mortgage payments for a bigger house, the bathroom with the rain shower and the Italian tiles – in order to be happy. Maybe these things will really make them happy, for a moment: but not half as happy as they would be if they walked free of the addiction.

I am happy. I sit on the shingle in the shelter of the sea wall, looking out across the ocean sparkling in the midsummer sun, and know that there is nothing more beautiful in the world. I snuggle down in bed at night beside the uncurtained window, gazing at the moon and the stars bright in the frosty sky, and the beauty of it almost calls my soul out of my body. I look at the glorious blossom of the Peace rose as it blooms in the tiny garden I reclaimed from the concrete, stoop to breathe in its fragrance, and my heart sings. I fetch wood from the pile under the plum tree, and start the fire ready for the household coming in weary at the end of the day; and I am so content. I watch my daughters, playing guitar and singing songs of praise to God, their long tresses of hair shining copper and brown in the lamplight, and I love them so much.

Even if it has not been your habit throughout your life so far, I recommend that you learn to think positively about your body.

Ina May Gaskin

If your morals make you dreary, depend upon it they are wrong. I do not say 'give them up,' for they may be all you have; but conceal them like a vice, lest they should spoil the lives of better and simpler people.

Robert Louis Stevenson

Really, it's a matter of programming our minds with the kind of information that will set us free.

Charles Swindoll

I weigh out flour and add herbs from the garden, salt from the sea, yeast and golden-green olive oil, honey and warm water, and begin to knead dough on the table in our kitchen for our daily bread. And I give thanks that God invited me to this rich and glorious life, to His party, to His way of joyous freedom and simplicity. I thank God that He has heard my prayer – He has given me my daily bread, the good grain of the way of simplicity.

Let the beauty that we love be what we do.

Jalal-Uddin Rumi

I love life, but I am ready to leave it at any moment. I am utterly content.

An interview with the author

Firstly, by way of introduction, tell us how you become a Christian and what made you decide to follow Christ?

There has never been a time when I did not believe in God. There has never been a time when I was not aware that 'here we have no abiding city'; and our true home is beyond this world, beautiful, holy and full of wonder though the earth most certainly is.

I was taken to church as a child by my mother, and the Christian faith influenced and underpinned the English culture in which I was raised.

Yet each of us has to choose for him/herself, and step knowingly into the way of Christ's Kingdom.

I was fifteen years old when I made that choice; invited Jesus into my heart to be the Lord of my life. I became His property on that day.

I was baptised in the Holy Spirit, entering into the Holy Spirit's charismata, a few weeks later, beginning to speak in tongues after reading Don Basham's book *Face Up With A Miracle*.

I think I decided to follow Christ because in His grace and humility He called me.

His presence flooded my soul with healing and joy, as I had heard others say that it would.

A couple of times that year I received laying-on-of hands ministry in which I was 'slain in the Spirit' as they say. Since then I've heard some folks speak about that kind of ministry with great suspicion. My testimony of it is, that it is the only time in my life when

I have felt simply okay; guilty about nothing, ashamed of nothing, anxious about nothing, no restlessness, no weariness. I just felt okay, and knew everything was okay: it was the sweetest state of being, and knowing that it is attainable and that it is reached through the ministry of Jesus gives me hope even still, more than thirty-five years later.

I was drawn towards seeking a personal relationship with the Lord Jesus by the joy I saw in His followers. I haven't seen that in a long time: and I miss it. Contemplating and cultivating joy is a discipline I have in view for my next task as a disciple. Joy is very healing and reconciling; it helps people get over things, and builds bridges where people are divided.

You spend much of your life pursuing the way of simplicity. Have you found other spiritual disciplines, such as fasting and meditation on scripture, to be helpful also? Why has simplicity had such an impact on you above all else?

I think you mean fasting from food, don't you? Yes, prayer with fasting is very powerful, and moves things along startlingly. But there are other kinds of fasting too, and that is part of what simplicity is. I fast from television a lot, because though I enjoy it, it is often debilitating to my soul. I fast from human company because I get carried away and talk too much, forgetting the recollection of the spirit that I ought to remember (Avoid godless chatter, because those who indulge in it will become more and more ungodly. 2 Timothy 2:16). I fast from status and trying to look clever or big (not a great renunciation in my case, as these things have not often been within my grasp – but they sometimes have been). The thing I fast from least is food because, in choosing simplicity and the discipline of a quiet and frugal life, food is allowed and keeps me cheerful.

I am a weak and flawed person, but it is my desire that my whole life should become a meditation on Scripture. That's the point of living simply – a Christian person's daily life is their meditation on Scripture.

I am not a great reader. I haven't read many books. I don't read quickly or prolifically, and I get bored if the books are abstruse or longwinded – for which reason I have read hardly any theology books.

I love the Bible, and I think hard about what it says; and I love the Book of Life – everyday reality, the natural world, what I see when I keep my wits sharp and my eyes open.

I have noticed that the Bible says simplicity is imperative – '...any of you who does not give up everything he has cannot be my disciple.' (Luke 14:33) – and I have noticed that in the Book of Life nobody makes progress in any spiritual path of any description without going through the door of simplicity. It isn't optional.

Living simply recognises that, though it doesn't mean beating yourself up or never having treats. It's just that, as Toinette Lippe says, 'Problems arise when things accumulate'; so it helps to accepts the kind of disciple that allows a person to remain spacious, flexible and free.

Your lifestyle could be described as fairly monastic – do you think it has led you toward people or away from them?

Fairly monastic? Ooh! You would have to ask my husband about that!

It's a fair question though, and an accurate observation. I love the spirituality of the monastic way, and have learnt so much about the daily rhythms of practical spirituality from monks and nuns with whom I have visited, conversed, lived, worked and worshipped.

One of the things I learned from monks and nuns is that you can spend much time in solitude and silence and still uphold human society and the lives of others in intercession, wrapping them in love that makes a difference.

A common mistake is to think that monastic enclosure removes people from society, when in fact it frees people to become society's beating heart of prayer, humility, service and love, holding fast to the hem of Christ's garment for the healing of us all.

My own life is lived in response to the question 'What was I sent here to do?' I regard my time as an unutterably precious treasure on loan to me from God; it is mine to steward but not to waste. That question ('What was I sent here to do?') leads me sometimes into the company of others and sometimes into solitude: but if my life is responding wisely and faithfully to that question, it will always lead me into love.

You have made some radical choices in search of simplicity. How do you find people react to this and to your lifestyle in general?

How people really react and how I imagine they react may be two different things. My answer to this reflects what I imagine.

First, I think very few people react to my choices at all. I live a very retired and solitary life; very few people know me or spend time with me, very few people have ever discussed with me my choices and the rationale that underlies them.

Those people who do spare a thought for my life, in the main, I imagine find me disappointing. I have made choices – leaving the ordained ministry for example – to do with integrity and simplicity that were probably not understood.

The choices I have made have sometimes caused others distress – parting with possessions and walking away from affluence do not seem immediately helpful in the world as we know it today. I could be seen as wasteful and unappreciative, I guess; because I rarely keep anything.

Has this been difficult for you, encouraging or both?

I am often lonely for the encouragement of others walking the same path. I have been moved and humbled by the willingness of my husband to accommodate my need to pare our belongings held in common right down to the bone, and to live in a shed. It's unusual, I grant you; he is a remarkable man.

God has called many Christians into the world of politics and business and their work is complicated and busy. It may also be well paid. Where is the path of simplicity, when life is so demanding and yet you feel God has called you to that life?

Two role models that come to my mind here are Mohandas Gandhi and Cardinal Basil Hume.

Gandhi's room at Mani Bhavan shows us how complicated it is necessary for an international politician to be.

Basil Hume held in balance the tension between the desert and the marketplace, which he saw as the twin centres of his calling: 'If I don't go into the desert, to meet God,' he said, 'then I have nothing to say when I go into the market-place'.

A life of simplicity can be very helpful in forming a mind that sees past unnecessary complication, and is not impressed by worldliness. The lessons of simplicity may even assist in achieving greatness. Abraham Lincoln may be a good example of this, raised as he was in a one-room log cabin by two uneducated farmers.

His first campaign speech, when he was twenty-three, went: 'Fellow citizens, I presume you know who I am. I am humble Abraham Lincoln. I have been solicited by many friends to become a candidate for the legislature. My politics are short and sweet, like the old woman's dance. I am in favor of a national bank. I am in favor of the internal improvement system and a high protective tariff. These are my sentiments and political principles. If elected, I shall be thankful ; if not, it will be all the same.'

It was said of him: 'He appeared in every sense of the word like one of the plain people among whom he loved to be counted'.

I have read that on the day Lincoln gave his inaugural address as President, a man stood up in the assembly to interrupt him with the words: 'Mr. Lincoln, you should not forget that your father used to make shoes for my family'; and everyone laughed, but Lincoln replied: 'Sir, I know that my father used to make shoes in your house for your family, and there will be many others here... because the way he made shoes; nobody else can. He was a creator. His shoes were not just shoes, he poured his whole soul in it. I want to ask you, have you any complaint? Because I know how to make shoes myself; if you have any complaint I can make another pair of shoes. But as far as I know, nobody has ever complained about my father's shoes. He was genius, a great creator and I am proud of my father'.

Abraham Lincoln kept something of the simplicity of his boyhood about him throughout his life; it seems not to have hindered him.

You take inspiration from other religions,
quoting for example Lao Tzu and Mohammed.
To what extent do they inform your faith and
how would you address those of your readers
who feel apprehension about drawing upon such
areas?

Li Erh, who came to be known as Lao Tzu (which means 'Old Sage') lived about six hundred years before Jesus was born. Some of the concepts in his thinking would, I believe, have pleased Jesus very much – for example Lao Tzu's idea of 'the valley spirit', which is about overcoming through gentleness, lowliness and humility.

Mohammed of course came about a thousand years later – five hundred years after Jesus, so his teachings could more reasonably be seen as rivalling the teaching legacy of Jesus and the wisdom of the church.

My own feeling is that I am not so wise that I can afford to ignore the wisdom of others because their religious affiliations are different from my own.

When I was in the last year of High School, I read a book by Simone Weil, *Waiting on God*, in which I remember her as expressing the view that Christ is Truth before He is Christ; and I felt that she had identified something very important there. What I understand her to mean is that what it means to be Christ is to hold the nature of truth within himself – as Jesus said, 'I am the way, the Truth and the Life'. It follows from that, that if the truth in Christ is absolute and real, then we need never be afraid to seek after truth wherever we find it, for in His grace our search will ultimately lead us to Him.

It's said sometimes that 'all truth is God's truth' – there can't be a false truth, can there? And as God is the source and heart of truth, where we find truth, we touch something of God.

I have found that the wisdom and insights of world religions have enriched rather than threatened my faith: Jesus Christ is my lord and Master, and I would have it no other way.

You are working on another book at present called **On the Road of Blessing.** *Tell us a little bit about that.*

On the Road of Blessing is all about my belief that because everything is made by God, reality flows in a particular direction – the way of the will of God. The Bible shows us which way God's will flows. Because all reality is flowing that way, we can create the best outcome in all our circumstances if we align ourselves with that flow.

As we go through life, inevitably we shall face sorrow and adversity: and sometimes our souls will be imperilled by prosperity and success, so that we are most in danger just when we feel everything's going really well.

On the Road of Blessing looks at how to put in place what the Bible teaches, for people who would like their conduct and experience, in good times and bad, to be flowing in the direction of real life.